2/04

Praise for
What Would I Believe
If I Didn't Believe Anything

"Groff takes the unusual and highly beneficial step of leading the reader through some of the great secular and religious classics and also of encouraging guided reflections on key passages. This original approach enabled me to appreciate them in a wholly new way."
  —Harvey Cox, Hollis Professor of Divinity, Harvard University,
     author of *The Secular City* and *Common Prayers: A Christian's Journey Through the Jewish Year*

"In an age when many have lost confidence in conventional approaches to Christian faith and spirituality, Kent Ira Groff faces these concerns honestly and sympathetically and from that posture of wisdom and humility offers fresh insights and inspiration for those at the crossroads or roadside of faith's journey. This book is a welcome resource for seekers and doubters and those who care about them."
  —Nathan D. Baxter, former dean, Washington National Cathedral

"If you are piecing together your spiritual roots, as many of us are today, this is the place to start. A wise, open-minded vision of what it means to embrace the spiritual life comes through Groff's work."
  —Lauren Artress, author, *Walking a Sacred Path: Rediscovering the Labyrinth as a Spiritual Tool,* canon for special ministries, Grace Cathedral, San Francisco

"Today people hunger for meaning and direction as perhaps never before, yet the assurances offered by traditional religions and philosophies have become hollow for many. Kent Ira Groff meets this dilemma head-on. This is solid writing grounded in intuition and intelligence, on the most vital questions we humans ever confront. This book is a spiritual compass pointing toward a richer, more fulfilling life for anyone fortunate enough to read it."
  —Larry Dossey, M.D., author, *Healing Beyond the Body, Reinventing Medicine,* and *Healing Words*

"This book is a cornucopia overflowing with spiritual adages, insights, practices, and prayers culled from many sources. . . . There is sure to be some fruit or flower that will nurture you here."

—Wendy M. Wright, chair of humanities, Creighton University, Omaha, Nebraska, and author, *Seasons of a Family's Life*

"With Kent Ira Groff as a guide, seekers—skeptical or earnest—are likely to glimpse unexpected connections between the mundane and the Holy that stir the embers of the soul and disclose pathways to faith that for many have become obscure—but remain longed for."

—Sharon Daloz Parks, author, *Big Questions, Worthy Dreams: Mentoring Young Adults in Their Search for Meaning, Purpose, and Faith*

"This is a book for seekers who are longing to find their way home, those weary of religious platitudes yet awed by beauty, truth, and the ultimate mystery of God. Kent Ira Groff offers not a road map but a compass that points the way for his readers' own journeys. With this rich tapestry of ideas as inspiration, Groff invites readers to find community with fellow pilgrims and to embrace the divine mystery that is the source of life."

—Martha J. Horne, dean and president, Protestant Episcopal Seminary in Virginia, and former president, Association of Theological Schools in the United States and Canada

"The author writes well, poking fun and prodding the reader to consider different angles and visions. Rather than making a legal argument, Groff paints on a canvas and asks us to step back and take a good long look at it."

—Michael Long, assistant professor of religion at Elizabethtown College in Pennsylvania, director of peace and conflict studies program, and author, *Have the Time of Your Life: Live for God in Each Moment* and *Creative Living: Martin Luther King Jr. and the Good Life*

WHAT WOULD I BELIEVE IF I DIDN'T BELIEVE ANYTHING?

A Handbook for Spiritual Orphans

A SPIRITUAL COMPASS TO POINT YOU HOME

KENT IRA GROFF

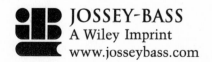
JOSSEY-BASS
A Wiley Imprint
www.josseybass.com

Published by Jossey-Bass
A Wiley Imprint
989 Market Street, San Francisco, CA 94103-1741   www.josseybass.com

Jossey-Bass books and products are available through most bookstores. To contact Jossey-Bass directly call our Customer Care Department within the U.S. at 800-956-7739, outside the U.S. at 317-572-3986, or fax 317-572-4002.

Jossey-Bass also publishes its books in a variety of electronic formats. Some content that appears in print may not be available in electronic books.

Library of Congress Cataloging-in-Publication Data
Groff, Kent Ira.
What would I believe if I didn't believe anything?: a handbook for
spiritual orphans / Kent Ira Groff.
p. cm.
Includes bibliographical references.
ISBN 0-7879-6758-0 (alk. paper)
1. Spirituality. I. Title.
BV4501.3.G76 2003
248.4—dc22   2003015406
Printed in the United States of America
FIRST EDITION
HB Printing   10 9 8 7 6 5 4 3 2 1

CONTENTS

HOW SHALL WE THEN LIVE? Having Fun Doing Good   145

LIST OF REFLECTION EXERCISES

*With gratitude
for the gift of
my son, Jim,
my daughters, Kendra and Beth,
their husbands, Chris and Dave,
and my grandson, Ian David Geddes,
and with burning hope
for the new generation*

ACKNOWLEDGMENTS

My life is lived in a web of community. I call the people listed here "acknowledgmentors," for I acknowledge each as a mentor in this writing journey: Mark Altschuler, Ted Anderson, Elizabeth Baker, Libby Werenfels Caes, Rabbi Carl Choper, Edward Craft, Daniel Dandy, Gordon De La Vars, Julia Esquivel, Roy Howard, Ray Lindquist, Michael Long, Patty Lowe, Jill Mallios, Scott McMillan, Stephen Melton, Thulani Ndlazi, John Norman, Marc Oehler, Luciano Picchio, Rabbi Phillip Pohl, Robert P. Richardson, John Sivley, Luther Smith, Edward Tyson, Keith Wilson, and my barber Laurie Young.

Kudos go to my wife and soulmate, Fredrika, for our many conversations and for her encouragement. Always I value the interchange of ideas with my daughters, Beth and Kendra, and my son, Jim. Especially I thank my cousin Paul Groff for the lens of his perceptions and his care. I am also blessed with countless young adults who gave me the gift of taffy-pulling exchanges and life-giving stories. (For the sake of confidentiality, I have changed names and a few details in our conversations.)

I am grateful to my editors, Julianna Gustafson and Andrea Flint, for their encouragement, carefulness, and insights. The English poet priest John Donne, despite his lover's quarrel with religious institutions of his day, knew so well that "no one is an island entire of itself." I hope the reader is blessed with the same quality of community as this writer has enjoyed.

Camp Hill, Pennsylvania   Kent Ira Groff
November 2003

ORIENTATION
Global Orphans

Today's spiritual topography has changed. Our elders cannot say "Here is the map for your faith"—because no one has ever charted faith in a twenty-first-century global environment. *Journey Without Maps,* Graham Greene's account of his trek through West Africa in the 1930s, parallels many seekers' "postmodern" spiritual journey—one that lacks fixed points for orientation.

DOES GOD EXIST?

Maybe I was a bit postmodern back in 1957 when the Soviet Russians came back from orbiting the first spaceship, *Sputnik.* They announced they had not found God, but I was not upset; it had never occurred to me that God was up there or out there.

"Does God exist?" has ceased to be a big deal for many of us. It sounds like looking for a God out there some*where,* or looking for heaven some*place.*

Rather, the big question is this: "Is God real?" This is the issue raised on the day space shuttle *Columbia's* crew died, and on the day my only brother died at age thirty-one. The way to test that Reality is to turn to the most crucifying realities of life and see if you can still detect even a thread of Love there.

We are all looking for some sort of homing thread in a "string theory" world where the tapestry threatens to unravel. My own string theory world began to unravel in 1987, during a crisis when a lifetime vocational dream disintegrated. Since childhood, I had dreamed of becoming a minister, but I never thought of anything but a traditional church with a square pulpit. Out of the cauldron of church conflict, painfully and over time there emerged a new congregation: my retreat ministry, and the new pulpit of my writing. But since then, it has been harder to *believe* in the traditional sense—that is, to get security from traditional doctrines or church structures. Even so, I have been carried into a deeper experience of faith and new forms of community.

Maybe you grew up in a faith community and left. Or left and returned. Or you may not think you are religious, yet you consider yourself a spiritual person. You may have experienced a leap of faith, or a slow walk into faith. You may be a religious leader but wondering how to preach on Easter after reading the latest "Jesus research." Or you question the value of faith, with so much hatred going on in God's name.

A COMPASS FOR GLOBAL ORPHANS

Everyone is orphaned, even unawares. In the United States all of us beautiful *and* ugly Americans (as Mark Twain tweaked us) are resident aliens: Anglo-Saxon types leaving behind European ancestries; Native Americans disinherited from ancestral geography in endless trails of tears; African Americans kidnapped from Africa and imported as slaves; Asians and Latinos, Jews and Arabs, illegal aliens and failed CEOs.

> Streams of children are literally orphaned as the AIDS plague takes their surviving parent in Africa and Asia, Australia and the Americas. More than half the children in the United States are separated from at least one parent by death, divorce, or other circumstances.

We now encounter this orphaning process globally. I

return to Kent County, England (my ancestral home), and Chester County, Pennsylvania (my childhood home), and visit farmers and townsfolk orphaned from their peaceful landscapes by megafarms, superhighways, and malls. Kids have to leave home to find jobs, while their elders gather in graying houses of worship and go bowling alone.

In Guatemala, Pedro and Maria used to eke out a living picking coffee. Now they are left behind, along with Señora Dona, a once-wealthy cardamom plantation landlord, since coffee and spice markets shifted to southern Asia.

As I eat with my fingers in the Indian home of my Princeton classmate Thomas and his wife, Anita, they tell me with pathos of their grandchildren far away in the United States with their son and daughter, physicians James and Sandya. Their voices echo myriad left-behind parents whose children now live far away from their ancestral roots in Kenya or Korea to make a new life in the United States or the United Kingdom— or far from an Ohio Amish farm to work in Silicon Valley, California. It is hard to tell who is more orphaned, the young people or their elders.

Ministers feel orphaned too. I no longer feel part of the other pastors' shoptalk since I am in a specialized ministry. I feel orphaned in my changing beliefs as well. When I mentioned this over lunch, a woman pastor and a black seminary professor said, "We feel that way all the time."

"Orphan"—the last word in Herman Melville's classic *Moby Dick*—includes each of us. We are all Ishmael, born of Abraham and his "foreign" wife, Hagar, Sarah's slave girl, who represents our own partly Muslim, partly Christian, partly Jewish rainbow coalition. After Captain Ahab's great ship *Pequod* (established religion) is wrecked, each of us Ishmaels is floating at sea. Then the roaming ship *Rachael* (marginalized religion) drifts by in search of her missing children and finds "another orphan."

We read about our orphaned selves in Anne Tyler's *Dinner at the Homesick Restaurant*. We see the film *Cider House Rules*

> We are also exiled from our ancestors' stories, leaving parts of our souls forgotten.

and feel a lot like the fake physician pretending to care for the world's lost orphans. Who is more orphaned? Who is more lonely: the pretend professional or the abused child?

This book is a compass for all who have a gnawing spiritual homesickness but are not at home in religious institutions. It is also for anyone within a community who wants to reach out to learn from seekers and also dares to reach into the doubting parts of his or her own soul.

HOW THIS HANDBOOK CAN WORK FOR YOU

Think of this book as my inviting you into a museum: you may glance at spiritual artifacts briefly in one room, feel drawn to music in others, or linger and gaze at a still life. You leave to take a bit of perspective into the world, and return later. I hope you will not just read these pages but also reflect and share your experiences.

You can make this happen by using the "Reflection Exercises" to engage in day-to-day practices to explore the mystery at the heart of your life. You can also try to meet with a few other pilgrims who are willing to ask, "How shall we then live?" To delve deeper, use the chapter notes in the back.

Community and practices can take lots of forms. Read the book alone, or along with a friend. . . . Either way, keep a journal to reflect and converse about your stirrings. . . . Use it as a

> Have fun doing good—whether playing with Pascal's idea of faith as a "wise wager" or trying out new ways to love your neighbor.

resource to spawn a small group, renew an existing group, or plan a retreat.

Congregations, college campuses, libraries, and continuing education retreat centers might host a gathering of once or maybe believers. Suggest that people invite grandkids, along with an aunt or a neighbor's nephew, and meet together to understand each other's common hopes and hungers. Prison groups might use the book as a resource for multicultural spiritual conversations.

As an option for any gathering, break into groups of two to six and share the Reflection Exercises, and then gather again as a whole. Be comfortable with silence, and find some rituals of closure (see Resource One at the end of the book).

HELPFUL HINTS FOR KEEPING A JOURNAL

Keeping a journal benefits personal and group life. I will coach you along the way with props such as the Reflection Exercises; they make good grist for journaling. Some people use a computer, yet I find writing longhand taps creative art and primal energies.

Use your journal to reflect on conversations or events or dreams or scriptures, to enter poetry or art (your own or others'). Use pastel colors. Glue things in it: a leaf, a feather, an e-mail note from a friend, a quote from an article. Insert sticky notes generously; jot down a dream fragment or an insight recalled at midday, a concern or a yearning.

I joke about making only two rules: first, date each entry; and second, make a mistake in the first one! Trying to say things right is a big barrier. Another is missed days, so I aim for four days out of seven.

Probably the biggest barrier to journaling is being too self-critical, writing out of the head instead of the heart. To break through the impasse, I suggest a simple method. Open to a clean page in your journal. Let your eye fall on an object in the room where you're sitting. Contemplate it for one minute. Then begin to write words or phrases *down* the page (instead of complete sentences from left to right). Once when I was leading a workshop in a federal prison, one man wrote:

Air vent in ceiling, high
like prison walls
Air inside confined
mixes with
air outside free.
Breathing in this air, I am
free inside.

I invite you to try this method to jumpstart your own journaling.

Reflection Exercise 1. Reader Response Format

Here is a method to practice a kind of meditative reading process with various types of books. This can serve as a catalyst to converse with a friend or partner if you read a book in common (using different color pens), or for group or class use. You may make actual notations in the margins, or just keep the three categories in mind:

! = Amen! (The author puts my own thoughts into words—
     think of the exclamation point!)
¡ = Aha¡ (Here's a light bulb, new insight—think of this sym-
     bol as a candle ¡)
? = Agnosticisms? (I'm not sure; this idea makes me struggle;
     it's fertile turf for learning; a question?)

CONVERSATIONS WITH SEEKERS
Genuine Experiences, Worthy Questions

I welcome you to listen in on conversations with a few doubting seeking friends. Many have experienced awakenings that silently inform their lives, yet mostly they keep them hidden from religious communities and the world. They raise worthy questions that we will explore.

> Across from me on the aisle seat is Mark, vice president for development for a local public radio station. He tells me how, growing up in Minnesota, he was a leader with Presbyterian youth, locally and nationally. He mentions Robert Putnam's book *Bowling Alone* and how his generation listens to NPR but they do not join. Married, with young children, he says, "I'm not involved in a church, but I still consider myself a spiritual person."

I invite you to look at life from below, exploring experiences and questions themselves rather than doctrines from above—and then relate them to live traditions. I call this a "method of correspondence." You need no prior theology. You are the curriculum. Maybe you recall a brief moment that redirected your life in an ordinary time of work or duty.

Over lunch, Jason tells me how he grew up with a smattering of Protestantism and a bigger dose of patriotism, which led him into the army. While stationed near Guantanamo Bay, Cuba, a transforming experience occurred one night when a large group of Cubans appeared. They could have killed the small band of American troops, but instead the "enemy" walked away, saving Jason and his petrified little group. His life changed, and he is still trying to make sense of it all by practicing meditation and giving back through public service. He has no connection with a community of faith.

I will be your coach for this method, as you explore real-life events like Jason's, and then look for corresponding analogies of faith in film and literature, psychology and science, poetry and arts, music and sports.

Steve, a nonobservant Jew born of Holocaust survivors, teaches American literature in college. His hobby is sports, especially baseball and tennis. He enjoys life, has deep compassion for marginalized people, questions the reality of God, and despises religious hypocrisy. Nevertheless, he is always pointing out subtle moments of grace in wild novels and short stories, movies, and life.

You can reframe even violence or abuse to reclaim life-giving connections and spiritual meanings. In this way, as with Tyrone, no drop of experience is ever wasted.

Tyrone's father killed his mother when Tyrone was seven. His negative way of coping was to act out, experimenting with the feeling of power. As an adolescent, one day recently while visiting his father in prison Tyrone found the courage to ask the question he always wanted to ask: "Why did you kill my mother?" In that moment, he discovered the power of feel-

> By valuing questions as the edge of faith, you can discover qualities of the sacred in fresh, nonreligious language.

ing, as his father did nothing but weep during an entire visit. Tyrone is now asking deeper questions about life, trying to understand his newfound meaning.

Mine the treasures buried in the raw material of your own experience. I draw from my own Christian well, sometimes painfully, but I also draw from other spiritual traditions. We tap a common underground stream beneath particular religions.

I picture Melissa, a bright business entrepreneur who grew up Catholic, yet along the way she was wounded in significant relationships. Now deeply involved in various alternative methods of healing and new age practices, she is struggling to make connections with her Christian roots as she explores Celtic spirituality.

Why do people find meaning in spirituality outside of organized religion but still have a yen to explore their own tradition?

Tanasha confides how she met Christ in her teens through a Pentecostal church. But when she discovered she was lesbian, she soon found herself alienated from her family and church— and the "Christ" who she was told condemns her. For years she struggled to change. Now, rediscovering the Christ who accepts her unconditionally, she is on a "sabbatical" from churchgoing, experiencing rejection whenever she tries to be part of one. Even so, she yearns for spiritual community.

Believers feel exiled, while many religious leaders feel stuck. "Faithless Faith Worker" reads ethicist Randy Cohen's column in a recent *New York Times Magazine,* about a clergyperson who's now an atheist.

I have just met with Dana, who, after preaching a sermon and while standing at the door to greet the congregation, had a flash thought: *If I weren't a pastor, I wouldn't go to church.*

I hope folks who are homesick to believe, but for whom institutional religion is a barrier, will say, "Ah, I'm not alone. Other souls put words to my feelings, give voice to my thoughts."

How can a genuine spirituality speak to those who appear strong in our culture but who actually feel powerless in the face of global complexity?

Will is in top management in a communications company. His team received awards for excellence in productivity and human relations. Still, as the pressure of global competition mounts, Will tells me people are being jerked right and left, fired, or reassigned without consultation, to save face for the company. Morale hit an all-time low, and the company finally filed for bankruptcy. He stays on, believing he is there to represent a human face every day in a cutthroat atmosphere that's a lot like the *Dilbert* comic series. He tells me he is beginning to pray again.

Despite the uniqueness of each one's quest, these people all share a subtle, or not-so-subtle, longing to listen beneath the surface of life. They are you—or your children, grandchildren, or friends. We are engaged in a sleuthing project, and if you join our detective trek we will explore how obstacles to faith, or even rebellion against religion, can be a worldly path to creativity and compassion.

THE GIFT IN THE GRIT

Losing Your Religion to Find Your Faith

I can sometimes say, "I no longer believe, but I see."
—Brother Lawrence, The Practice of the Presence of God

Once in a while
you can get shown the light
in the strangest of places
if you look at it right.
—Robert Hunter for Jerry Garcia,
"Scarlet Begonias"

1

BEING AGNOSTIC CRACKS THE DOOR TO TRUTH

The opposite of faith is not doubt. The opposite of faith
is certainty. A person who claims to know the mind
or will of God is pathological.
—ALAN JONES, DEAN OF GRACE CATHEDRAL,
SAN FRANCISCO, NOVEMBER 2001

Every creative act involves . . . a new innocence of percep-
tion, liberated from the cataract of accepted beliefs.
—ARTHUR KOESTLER, THE SLEEPWALKERS

I n a moment of doubt, in the time between locking my car
door in the parking lot and using my electronic key to open
the lower-level door of the building where I teach, the key
elements of a spiritual crisis dropped into my awareness.

During the forty-five minute drive through the Amish
country of Pennsylvania, down I-283 from Harrisburg to Lancaster, I felt my vocational integrity disintegrating as mentor and
director of a spiritual development organization.

I have often pondered what happened that August morning. Back home after weeks away, I felt good that I started the
day by spending nearly an hour practicing physical and contem-

plative prayer. But I got anxious since I was then running late—and I snapped at my wife. She rejoined, "So what good does it do you to sit in there and meditate?" Her question exposed the tip of an iceberg of self-deceit. Adding to that the news of insane violence in the world, I felt emptied.

How could I live with the widening gap between the spiritual life I professed and the daily reality of emptiness I was experiencing? How could I dare to teach, converse with others, and write about it? How dare I not speak of it? It is *the* occupational hazard for spiritual leaders. It was as though my whole Christian house of cards was collapsing.

Getting out of my car, a thought occurred to me to make a sort of inner examination. Do I have anything left at the core, beneath this stripping down of faith, this loss of confidence? I heard myself ask: *What would I believe if I didn't believe anything?*

A question had become a key. In the space of a couple of minutes and a hundred or so yards, I realized I knew three things deeply, beneath any external creeds or beliefs.

The gift is in the grit. I knew any hoped-for glimpses of insight or joy, any primal homing instinct or peak experiences arise out of the crazy stuff of suffering and sex, boredom and beauty.

Wonder happens. I realized insight or hope cannot be programmed. The element of surprise seems to be part of some random cosmic wiring. Serendipity. Despite my attempts to control, a playful hound of heaven charges from behind and pops up ahead.

Mystery. In my mind I heard the echo of a student's words the week before: "You should see Mt. St. Helens now!" The world is ablaze with inklings of transformation—mysterious hints of devastation and renewal in nature, in nations, and in my own life.

That night I entered these ideas in my journal (I still have it) almost the way you see them. Then a fourth emerged:

How shall we *then live?* I cannot change the world without *we.* What would it mean to listen to life in order to love . . . to contemplate truth, and act truthfully?

Over the next weeks, all four ideas raised questions more exciting than their solutions. I wondered: Could this stripping down of beliefs be an opportunity for deeper connection with the bare bones of faith—within myself, with particular doubting and seeking friends, and with "a-theists" (literally "non-godists") who reject a God I no longer believe in either?

It occurred to me that my agnostic moment in the parking lot contained a hologram for exploring the ocean beneath my own doubting believing quest. Reflecting in the deep of winter, now I struggle to write about things that seemed clearer in the summer. It was like knowing something deeply yet feeling less sure of external beliefs. As the seventeenth-century active mystic Brother Lawrence said, "I no longer believe, but I see."

> There is a whole worldview of difference between most religious leaders and younger seekers. Yet we can all meet on the common ground of needing to learn from each other. Together we get fresh direction from ancient truths.

A SPIRITUAL COMPASS: FOUR WORKING HYPOTHESES

I noticed that these four observations do not depend on explicitly religious language. As mentioned earlier, Graham Greene's image of *Journey Without Maps* speaks of a postmodern environment where people mistrust anyone claiming to have *the* truth. It is an atmosphere charged with particles of Einstein's relativity theory and Heisenberg's uncertainty principle, with everything now wound up in string theory—or threatening to unravel. So then I began to argue with myself: "How dare you put forth four 'universal' ideas for everyone?"

So I can't create a full-scale map. Instead, I offer a spiritual compass with its four directions bidding you to ask yourself where your life wants to lead you. Step into your own laboratory of experience and explore these four themes as working hypotheses.

Maps of previous generations can still be helpful, but they are more like the geographers' maps showing things before the great continental rifting took place—when Africa, humanity's birthplace, was still connected to the Americas and other continents. Or like using an outdated atlas instead of going online to get a route that is in the process of construction.

If you are under age forty and live in a "developed" country, you have grown up in a different cultural terrain. This creates a vacuum of understanding and experience for your elders. For example, only 8 percent of pastors in one major U.S. church denomination are under thirty-five. The number of Americans who say they do not belong to any religion has nearly doubled in the past decade, from 8 percent to 14 percent, or twenty-nine million people. A recent poll said that 77 percent of England's young people say they have no religious belief. The Barna Research Group reports that 72 percent of those born in the United States between 1964 and 1981 are not involved in a church community, creating a unique generation.

In this uncharted terrain, you take your compass and these four quadrants, and you enter into your own lab investigation. Think of magnetic north as our fourth theme: "How shall *we* then live?" We all want the good life. This one big question provides the orientation, even if you are off in a different direction exploring the other three quadrants. You get where you need to go by keeping your eye on primal north, even in the modern high-tech world. This is what I develop in Chapter Six as "primodern" spirituality.

A lab needs community; *I* cannot live fully without *we*. So be attentive to your heart's direction, but also test your experience with the observations of others, reflecting on sacred texts and community traditions over time. I picture groups gathering to volley with these ideas, being comfortable with meditative silences, and listening to one another.

Seekers are my teachers as I explore how obstacles to faith, and rebellion against religion, can lead to the real yearning beneath it all. I am learning how doubting can be the opening for a new kind of faith. Like the emperor moth struggling to emerge from a chrysalis that once kept it safe but now constricts it, the *gift* is in the *struggle.*

Believing too easily or too rigidly can shut out truth that can liberate individuals and institutions. This story from the Buddha illustrates the dangers of holding one's beliefs too tightly.

> While a young widower is away on business, bandits burn his village. On returning, the widower finds the remains of a dead child near his former house. Assuming it is his own son, after proper cremation ceremonies he carries the remains with him at all times, continually grieving. But in fact his son has been kidnapped. One night the real son escapes and comes to his father's new house, pounding on the door, "Papa, it's me, open the door." "But," the father insists, "you cannot be my son; my son is dead." He will not open the door—and his son leaves, never to be embraced by his own father.

Genuine believing means being willing to give up preconceived ideas to open the door to truth. To really listen to your life, you need to be agnostic (literally, "unknowing").

Doubting believing can be a necessary prelude to rebuilding faith. Unbelieve in order to rebelieve. God is everywhere, even in the urge to rebel against God. Leaving home, you realize along the way that home left you.

Filled with preconceived beliefs, our ears are plugged—sometimes feeling too certain, sometimes feeling too cynical. Either way, the path from belief to new life lies in emptying our ingrained habit of mind.

Maybe it is sudden; maybe slow. Only through something akin to *The Cloud of Unknowing* (to quote the title of an anonymous medieval book) can we as individuals and institutions shed our certitudes, and really listen.

"Yada, yada, yada . . ." folks yodel, while they put one foot in front of the other, facing the daily grind of work and the grit of relationships. But in Hebrew, *yada* means "to know." Sometimes we get to what we really need to know by the repetitive boring things that lead us to a place of unknowing. This kind of agnosticism can be the dark place where the pupa of the old life incubates into a new kind of knowing.

Reflection Exercise 2. On Your Way Home with the Beatles (or Simon and Garfunkel)

Option A: Have your journal handy. Relax with a few deep breaths. . . . Listen to the Beatles' song "Two of Us," which opens their CD *Let It Be,* with its repeated refrain about being on our way home. Listen for other phrases or words that speak to you about trying to arrive but going nowhere. Reflect on any connections to your spiritual journey. (Lyrics from Capitol Records, Inc., USA; sound recording by EMI Records, England, 1970).

Option B: Listen to "Homeward Bound" on *The Best of Simon and Garfunkel.* Imagine your love life as the Love deeper than all human loves, waiting silently for you. (www.sonymusic.com/artists/SimonAndGarfunkel)

Reflection Exercise 3. One Moment of Direction—or Indirection

Take a few minutes in silence. . . . Scan your life, noting turning points, roads not taken, shifts in your thinking. Do you notice any key moment that redirected your life? Or that unleashed a crucial question of faith for you—a moment of indirection? Was it a line of conversation? a fleeting thought? a person encountered? a facet of nature? a dream? an experience of prayer or worship? Reflect in your journal. Can you think of someone with whom you feel drawn to share this experience?

2

BIG BARRIERS TO BELIEVING

Every time I tried to tell you,
the words just came out wrong.
So I'll have to say I love you in a song.
—JIM CROCE

My conversations with seeking friends can validate your own search. You may have been abused by institutional religion, as Melissa was—or found it boring. Or as Steve says, "It just seems wrong-headed, claiming to know answers via being the chosen people or via acceptance of Jesus, or whatever." You may be a spiritual leader in a religious institution, like Dana, and need a safe way to explore the edges of your own doubts. For others, it is an emotional and spiritual meltdown, as Michael Stipe sings in R.E.M.'s "Losing My Religion." Things fall apart; you say things that shock yourself and it sparks a crisis of integrity.

LOSING YOUR RELIGION

Sometimes you do not plan to lose your religion. Someone loses it for you. A drunk driver, an abusive representative of God, or

> You might think you have no religion to lose—that is, anything that consumes your ultimate passion—until you lose it and feel the emptiness.

a betraying lover suddenly turns whatever God you believed in upside down.

Sometimes it just happens, in the way a partly opened soda loses its fizz overnight. Actually, you may have lost your religion but not your *faith,* though others think you have. You may be experiencing a dark night of the soul—barely finding hints of the Presence, like stars on a foggy night—which I explore in Chapter Eighteen, on emptiness.

It can happen suddenly and gradually. Once, while a minister was preaching, a man suddenly laughed out loud, echoing the minister's own smoldering doubts. The incident led him to leave the local church—and, ironically, thrust him into a new vocation of teaching future ministers the art of people skills.

Or suddenly you wake up one morning and say, "I can't believe this stuff anymore." Questioning the "stuff" can be the catalyst for the journey back home. So if you can befriend the monsters of doubt and disillusionment, like Beauty finally embracing the Beast, they may become the first signs of reawakening.

It is scary to lose your religion. But in the process you may discover beneath it the thing you really treasure most—your true religion. "Those who find their life shall lose it, and those who lose their life for my sake will find it," runs one of Jesus' Eastern-like koans, or riddles. It might be paraphrased: "Lose your religion to find your life."

BIG BARRIERS

But is there any choice between fanatical fundamentalism and a complete spiritual meltdown? Engineers tell me a well-designed bridge requires flexibility as well as stability. A bridge that is too rigid does not give with the rigors of environmental stress. Here is a worthy vision for the spiritual quest: to be able to give even under stress.

How can we develop genuine faith, passionate *and* open to questioning itself, willing to shed its outgrown shell for a new creature to be born? We cannot go anywhere real unless we face the obstacles honestly. In naming barriers here, I raise big questions to validate your own struggles, which I explore in more depth throughout the book.

OUTDATED GODTALK

In Lake Wobegon, says Garrison Keillor, "All the Norwegians were Lutherans, of course, even the atheists—it was a Lutheran God they did not believe in." The theism a lot of atheists reject describes a God I cannot believe in either. Many grew up, as I did, with an emotionally or physically absent father, yet hearing of God mainly as a male figure—so no wonder God seemed distant. Images and language skew our attitude toward the sacred. Can a word such as "surrendering" to God perpetuate a distorted spirituality for a child, spouse, or worker who has submitted for too long to an abuser? Trusting in God is more like "yielding" to a cause greater than oneself.

THE BUDDHIST ON YOUR STREET

Our grandparents' faraway world is now in our living room, on our TV and computer screens. For centuries, missionaries were sent around the world starting schools and hospitals, though mainly, folks assumed, to convert "heathen" Buddhists, Muslims, Hindus, or animists. Now the Buddhist child next door is your son's best friend; Hindus convert a downtown church into a temple; Muslims are invited to explain their faith; and an atheist shovels snow from the widow's driveway down the street.

THE END OF OTC (ONLY TRUE CHURCH)

"Church" is not the only place where people go for spiritual meaning and service. (Was it ever?) Yet many groups are founded on the OTC assumption. Like the culture, traces of authoritarian certitude and patriarchal structure persist even in religions trying to be inclusive. So if you will not go to hell for not being part of a religious institution, is there any other reason to engage in a spiritual quest? I am inviting you to explore your unique quest—and new forms of community.

"THE BIBLE SAYS SO"

Abuses among all religions repel thinking and compassionate people. Nevertheless, sixteenth-century reformers, aided by the printing press, made the Bible accessible and with it the free world of ideas, fostering the Enlightenment. But today fundamentalists freeze medieval doctrines, instead of continuing the reformation. Literalists in all religions wrench a few damaging words out of context and cancel the scriptures' timeless message of love. At the same time, ordinary people devour scholars' biblical research, refreshed or puzzled by what is left of the Jesus they thought they knew. How can critical study prepare the way for building up faith? In my tradition, I speak of "journeying alongside the Jesus of history to the Christ of experience."

THE EXPLOSION OF KNOWLEDGE

In an Internet age, we experience information overload and fragmentation. Having myriad specialists, it is hard to keep up with the whole field, be it health or religion, economics or literature. It is even harder to integrate so many other burgeoning specialties. The poet John Donne describes our time: "T'is all in peeces, all cohaerence gone." The multiplicity of stimuli makes it difficult to practice simplicity, what the spiritual traditions call a "single eye." Can we live contemplatively in a complex world?

THE SACRED-SECULAR SPLIT

I am writing out of a passion to bridge this worldly-versus-holy divide. For me, this means taking the Incarnation seriously: "The Word became flesh." Our fleshy nature can be a vehicle for the spiritual. *Passion* conveys sexuality but also suffering, as in Jesus' passion and violent death. Still, there is a stained glass split between sexuality and spirituality, violence and values. All of them come together in a movie such as *The Shawshank Redemption* (based on a Stephen King novel): the innocence of a white banker on death row, the sex scandal that caused his wrongful conviction, and his redemption through a black prisoner. Discussing such a film can be sacramental.

SUFFERING

How can a Supreme Love allow suffering? People often misquote the title of Harold Kushner's popular book *When Bad Things Happen to Good People* as Why *Bad Things Happen . . . to Good People.* We want answers. But Kushner did not try to figure out *why* suffering happens. Rather, *when* it happens, how do we respond creatively instead of destructively? What kind of God can we believe in since the Holocaust? Vietnam? 9/11? Iraq?

> **Collateral Damage**
> FRIENDLY FIRE KILLS INNOCENTS
> "War is hell," the General said.
> I wonder, God, if you are dead.
> Or can it be that where you dwell
> is just within such living hell?

Could what people mean by God be the mysterious bits and pieces of love swirling around within the suffering itself?

LACK OF PERMISSION TO QUESTION—OR SHARE EXPERIENCES

Many people do question. But they feel orphaned if they try to express their skepticism or scientific worldview, their anger or spiritual abuse in religious institutions—or to God. Ironically, people who have mystical experiences also fear rejection if they speak of the occasions within the walls of a religious structure.

A child, abused nightly, may have a vision of Jesus standing in the room, protecting her. So often a spiritual vision lies close, in the psyche, to an experience of submerged pain; it is hard to speak of one without the other.

BORING RELIGION

Seekers want to *experience* something they do not have the name for. Instead, many religious folks talk about a God that seems out of touch, often mouthing damaging phrases, such as "It's God's will," at the scene of a car crash. William James quipped, "Faith is either a dull habit or an acute fever." Is there anything in between?

VIOLENCE CAUSED BY RELIGION

The ultimate turnoff is when a community teaches love but believes so intensely that it harasses or even kills anyone who differs. Osama bin Laden reportedly claimed God attacked the United States on September 11, 2001, killing citizens from many countries. While rescuers were still at work, TV evangelist Jerry Falwell said God was punishing America for homosexuality and abortion—though he later apologized. Both Gods seem vicious or stupid. A little healthy doubt can temper a dangerous certitude. Yet who wants a boring faith?

A human emergency can be the occasion for spiritual emergence.

How can you experience genuine faith and live it out passionately—without a crusade mentality? Somewhere between wallowing in spiritual apathy and fleeing to dangerous religion, we catch a clue: the true grit of ordinary barriers can create a bridge to a deeper level of faith.

THE BRIDGE FROM CREED TO DEED

As Jim Croce sang, ". . . the words just came out wrong" when trying to communicate love. The biggest Godtalk barrier is when believers' deeds do not match their creeds. Young people, says Lauren Winner, a popular young writer who recently became Christian, "are not so much wary of institutions as wary of institutions that don't do what they are supposed to do." Shopworn language is an invitation to create fresh images and institutions that embody the words they proclaim. Rebbe Nachman of Breslov speaks to this:

> There are people who after a whole lifetime of materialism suddenly feel a strong desire to walk in the paths of God. The attribute of judgment then rises up to accuse them. It tries to prevent them following the way of God by creating barriers. The unintelligent person, when seeing these barriers, starts to back away. But someone with understanding takes this as the very signal that one should draw closer. That person under-stands that God is to be found in the barrier itself—and the truth is that Godself is indeed hidden in this barrier.

The summer before my sophomore year at Penn State, a class-mate called to tell me of a conference in New Hampshire, something like "true faith for times like these." It was free, a farm kid's ideal vacation. But it turned out to be a "Christian right" camp, with actual lists of mainline church ministers branded "communists." I felt my soul gripped in a vice of fear. What saved me from imbibing hate that felt like hell was telling myself a verse in the first letter of John: "There is no fear in love, but perfect love casts out fear." From that point in my life, I involved myself in causes for peace and justice. The barrier became a bridge.

AVOIDING THE TWIN ROADS TO HELL

While I was writing this book, a friend challenged me: "Why do you have such a passion to write this book if you, a minister,

> What if instead of dodging the obstacles we turned toward them? We might begin to detect bits and pieces of grace in the grit, bridging the sacred-secular split.

don't think people are going to hell if they're not in a church?" I recalled the story of the radical right camp, and together we affirmed two reasons: rigid exclusiveness creates a hell on earth, and individualist love without community is powerless to create a loving person or peaceful world.

So how can you avoid these twin roads to hell on earth: clutching rigid beliefs to get a quick fix of security or falling for an anything-goes individualism? Here is a foundation thread woven throughout this book: by following your soul's path with some fellow pilgrims, rather than alone, you become a more loving and genuine person, and more aware of beauty in the brokenness in the world.

Reflection Exercise 4. Losing Track of Time: Contemplation Unawares

When was a time you looked at something or some person with so much love that you lost track of time? Meditate on the experience, revisiting the feelings. Now ask, what are the qualities of such an experience? If you are in a group, you need not share the experience itself (if it is too personal), but pay attention to the qualities people mention.

Reflection Exercise 5. Barriers to Believing, Edges of Growth

By yourself, or in a group, open your journal to two clean pages. Reflect on obstacles that make it hard to believe, writing what you do *not* believe (on the left page), then what you are learning in relation to it (on the right page). Afterward, share your responses with a group, or another person. Here are two examples, with global and personal dimensions:

Barriers: Things I don't believe.	*Growth: Things I am learning.*
I don't believe religions should fight each other.	I decided to learn about the world's religions. I'm hoping for a Hindu friend.
I don't believe God causes cancer.	Being with my dying friend, I am learning how fragile life is.

3

HIDE AND SEEK IN STUFF

By virtue of the Creation and, still more, of the Incarnation,
nothing here below is ever profane to those who
know how to see.
—Pierre Teilhard de Chardin, The Divine Milieu

I am deeply interested in the way "God talk" enters
"street work."
—Arlene Helderman, "Spiritual Orphan"

Matt, thirty-something and the youngest resident in a nursing home, burst forth in a diatribe of rage. Just then I happened to enter the building and got the message *Chaplain, go directly to Matt. Do not pass Go.* (Matt had sustained traumatic brain injury from a car crash two decades ago after a high school graduation party.)

Spontaneously, I kneeled beside his wheelchair as he pounded his fists on the lap tray, yelling his favorite word. Looking directly into his face, I found myself saying: "Matt, you're really smart! You were accepted at Notre Dame. How do you spell that word?" He paused, then began saying each letter, rapid-fire, "S–H–I–T! S–H–I–T! S–H–I–T!" suddenly punctuated by gales of laughter.

TRACES OF GRACE IN THE GRIT

What happened? I pondered. How did Matt's red-hot anger metamorphose in seconds into humor? This tiny piece of learning represents a hologram of greater transformations. I noticed how I had *not* attempted to silence Matt's "shit" but instinctively entered into it more deeply, kneeling, conveying affirmation, and giving him a way to analyze the image's intensity by breaking it down into parts. It happened as an intuitive reflex, not a conscious plan.

I believe Matt and I were participating in a moment of awe enfleshed in raw human experience—what Christians mean by Incarnation (we become Christ's body), akin to what Hindus mean by an *avatar* (a little incarnation of the God Vishnu), not just ages ago but now. Forgetting any words in my books and seminars on anger, I found in that instant "the Word became flesh and tented among us," embodied in Matt and me. That miniature event offered a clue for developing Matt's longer-term goals.

O PLAYFUL LIGHT!

In Matt's story, hilarity and humor come very close to the *sacred* and its dyslexic cousin *scared*—since anger feeds on fear. Whenever pieces of humor emerge from the terrifying events of life, we are near some great mystery. A capsule of grace drops into our confinement, and for a moment something in us is freed. *Humor* lies down close to the bottom of life, hence its seeming connection to *humus* and *humility.*

A comedian's humor often develops out of the pain of physical and verbal putdowns as a child. Truth may lie dormant

I hope you can reframe what you thought were only "secular" experiences, to see pinholes of a spiritual eclipse ("I may actually be on a spiritual journey")—though it might have been too bright to see directly at the time.

until jolted loose by what traditions call a "holy fool" —Kokopeli of the Zuni Pueblo Native Americans, Nasrudin among Sufis—or the "poor fool" in Shakespearean drama, who is free to speak forth the truth.

Jesus embodies the "holy fool" in the Gospels: people complain about Jesus' Zen-like riddles (God has "hidden these things from the wise and the intelligent and [has] revealed them to infants"). This "messiah" fools away his time with riff-raff, bucks the religious and political establishment, and finally gets crucified on a garbage heap. Paul writes, "God chose what is foolish in the world to shame the wise"—a kingly fool on a cross, wearing a crown of thorns.

A host of Jesus' disciples follow in this path. St. Francis strips naked before the bishop to disown his father's wealth, and he kisses a leper. In Russia's well-known holy-fool tradition, clownlike mystics wore rags and slept on the streets or church porches. Stories are told how blessed sages like Basil would hurl stones at houses of self-indulgent rich folks and compassionately kiss the doors of prostitutes' houses. A little Albanian nun we know as Mother Teresa would kiss a man dying with maggots to offer "something beautiful for God" in Calcutta's slums.

Robert Hunter's lyrics in "Scarlet Begonias," quoted earlier, express light's mysterious secret: "Once in a while you can get shown the light / in the strangest of places if you look at it right."

I have just finished saying the Episcopal office of Evening Prayer, which includes an ancient hymn still listed in Greek as *Phos Hilarion* ("O Gracious Light . . ."—literally "O hilarious light"). I like to translate it as "O playful light."

It is as if the light plays hide and seek. The film *Life Is Beautiful* presents a tragic, amazing story where an Italian Jewish family become victims in the Holocaust, yet the power of play saves the son's life. At the beginning, the boy plays hide and seek under the covering of the family table at his birthday party. It is a playful rehearsal that foreshadows his serious hiding out later on in garbage cans and boxes, instructed by his father before he dies. After the Nazi troops flee the camp, the boy is rescued by friendly soldiers in a tank. Suddenly he sees his mother and calls out, "Mama, Mama!" The two are joyfully reunited. Mysteriously, hiding out becomes a way of seeking the light.

Even revolting images such as the Nazi horrors, in contrast to the hope in the film's title *Life Is Beautiful,* can evoke overpowering awe, as Rudolf Otto shows in his classic book *The Idea of the Holy.* Otto calls this numinous awe the *mysterium tremendum*—the tremendous mystery—with the repeated primal "om" sound, as in *shalom* and *home.*

Southern writer Flannery O'Connor evokes this life-in-death mystery. Her off-balance freaks, like the Misfit in "A Good Man Is Hard to Find," enable us to experience lightness of being through irreverence and violence in the extremes of life. The Misfit says about the grandmother he has just shot, "She'd of been a good woman if it had been somebody there to shoot her every minute of her life." This story screams out: *Live this moment as if you were to die the next.* O'Connor's turbulent stories shake us and take us to the edges of life. Then we appreciate that life *is* beautiful at the center.

Our spiritual seeking may be ignited by a human quest for self-understanding. I am thinking of thirty-five-year-old Sean, who was six when his father died. Sean contacted people like me who had known his father, to provide missing "snapshots." I responded by inquiring a bit more, and he e-mailed back:

> We stopped attending church when I was about 10. I never really went back, but still consider myself a spiritual person. My wife is Catholic and the difference between us is that I don't feel guilty about not attending church and she does! . . .

> The light plays hide and seek. Mysteriously. "We all have something to hide," says Mr. Meredith in the movie *Gosford Park*. We may hide out for years in the shadow of shame or suffering, until one day we begin to seek.

Turning 35 this year was a bit strange, as this was my father's age when he passed away. I thought I'd be struck with a sense of mission to 'make my mark' in some way. That hasn't happened. . . .

Maybe. But I predict Sean's search for his father's stories, which he recognizes as a key to his own identity, is already leading him on a spiritual journey where he will make his mark. It is an archetypal pattern of human experience: in the afternoon of life the shadow comes to the fore. After age thirty-five or so, Carl Jung would say, every question is really a spiritual question. The light plays hide and seek.

HIDE AND SEEK, YIN AND YANG

The hidden parts of yourself are an invitation to seek. If you have led a worldly life, now you begin looking for a spiritual spin to things. If your life has been focused mainly inward, now you begin moving outward into the world of action. If you never lacked for things, now you develop compassion for people with nothing. If you were protected, now you seek adventure. If as a child you were deprived, now you begin to claim your potential.

Like the Taoist yin and yang symbol, there may be only a little dot of dark in the light half, and a little light in the dark half, each needing its opposite. One begins to value feeling as well as thinking—or both at once. A young adult said to me, "I'm kind of right-brained and left-brained: I feel deeply about what I think about." Personality types differ, but spiritual wholeness means to begin embracing the shadow side of oneself.

Like chiaroscuro in a Rembrandt painting, the massive darks are essential to create the spare highlighted subjects. In

Yin and Yang

such fashion, things begin to integrate: secular and sacred, success and suffering, spirituality and sexuality, contemplation and action, security and adventure.

An old Latin phrase, *lacrimae rerum,* translated woodenly, means "the tears of things." It points to the underlying connection of all created things: emotional and material, persons and nature, spiritually interdependent.

The Lakota and other Native Americans understand this: *Mi taku ye oyasin!* means, "To all my relations!" It is like a toast to the living, the ancestors, the rocks and trees and animals. Likewise, in the Bible the divine is revealed through a burning bush or a stubborn jackass, a clay pot or a grapevine, a widow's penny or the face of a stranger, the wood of a manger and the wood of a cross.

That is what this theme is all about: tracking the grace in the true grit of experience. In Elizabeth Barrett Browning's words:

> Earth's crammed with heaven,
> And every common bush afire with God;
> But only those who see, take off their shoes—
> The rest sit round it and pluck blackberries,
> And daub their natural faces unaware.

HOLY HUMUS!

A woman on retreat was praying when she heard a construction worker say, "Holy shit!" Later she and I pondered, Can this pop

> The image of God as the "Ground of being," from the fifteenth-century mystic Meister Eckhart and popularized by the twentieth-century theologian Paul Tillich, offers an alternate view: from a God out there to God within the earthy ballast of our lives.

phrase mask our yearning for life's "waste" to become a source of wholeness and holiness?

We can take a cue from Luther's visceral spirituality; you find plenty of crass words and slang in *Luther's Table Talk* and personal prayers. So maybe people are "praying" without knowing it—praying that life's lowest places might be consecrated ("Holy humus!"). The expression can mean more than venting one's spleen. We will be learning (especially in Chapters Fifteen through Seventeen, on the matrix, beauty, and gesture) how to relinquish negative things to the Ground of our being to nurture other beautiful creatures.

Leaving
A leaf that has served its function
as a thing of beauty
can only become
nurturing humus
when it leaves:
detaching
as it grieves,
it fails and falls
to the Ground of its being
to nurture another thing of beauty.

Reflection Exercise 6. Beginning Prayer If You Can't Pray

People speak about not being able to pray. Religious language may get in the way. First, try substituting the word *yearn* for *pray*. What is it you really yearn for, beneath the things, experiences, or relationships you spend so much time on? Second, you would not be thinking about prayer if you didn't want to pray. So listen to your desire. That is your prayer. Ancient wisdom says, "Merely the desire to pray is already prayer."

4

THE "VULGAR" BIBLE

Purity is the ability to contemplate defilement.
—SIMONE WEIL, GRAVITY AND GRACE

Jerome gave the world a "vulgar" Bible, translating the original Hebrew and Greek scriptures into the Vulgate (common) Latin of the fourth century. The New Testament was written in common *(koiné)* Greek, not classical. Luther followed suit in the sixteenth century, translating the Bible into Low German, believing that one should first listen to the woman in the street and the man in the field, and then translate the sacred text. This was also the goal of England's King James I; in his authorized version of the Bible in 1611, "thee" and "thou" in that era were familial forms of address. Thomas Cranmer compiled *The Book of Common Prayer* to create community by way of common forms of speech, and its revisions are still on the best-seller list.

How can faith today connect to the vulgar things around us? Here are some glimpses.

THE SIMPLE POWER OF TURNING

Desmond Tutu tells of brutal killers in South Africa who slowly cooked people alive at one end of a campsite while enjoying a barbecue at the other end. Later in the Truth and Reconciliation Commission hearings, these perpetrators would confess without emotion that they were sorry. They might be staring across the room or down at their shoes as they spoke. But if a victim's family member said, "*Turn* to me; now say what you just said," then the confessor would be deeply moved, hardly able to gasp the words.

In telling this story, the word *turn* becomes flesh; a simple human act of turning *embodies* spiritual power. This is exactly what the word *shuv* in the Hebrew Bible means: "turn," though it is usually translated "repent." The New Testament Greek word *metanoia* literally means "turning one's thoughts" or "changing one's mind." Yet when translated into English as "repentance" both words convey religious scruples and miss the basic human connection. The Bible *sounds* more religious than it really is.

If the victim in South Africa had said "repent to me" instead of "turn to me," it would have missed the vulnerable place in the perpetrator's heart. In this way, ordinary words and gestures can have more power than religious language.

Meanwhile, the radio preacher goes on pounding the pulpit: "Repent!" We go right on driving to the mall to buy clothing made with child labor in a sweatshop. The simple language of turning can embody more power than repenting. What if we actually *turned our thoughts* toward the sweatshops? Or *turned* toward the face of the clerk who sells us the discounted jeans? Or *turned* toward our real needs beneath our wants?

MINDFULNESS AND *SHEMA*: "PAY ATTENTION"

For each of us, our life is basically defined by what we pay attention to. Whatever occupies your dominant concern is your religion. This is why spiritual traditions of East and West teach that simple *awareness* creates spiritual momentum. It is the meaning of the Hebrew *Shema:* "Hear, listen, pay attention to Love . . . and you shall love. . . ."

This same word *Shema* is translated as "obey," but then again obedience sounds moralistic. This English word *obey* comes from the Latin *ob-audio,* meaning "listen toward." And "acoustics" comes from the New Testament Greek *hyp-acouo:* "listen beneath." Here is a liberating message for our audio culture swimming in acoustical guitars and amplifiers: *Listen beneath the surface of life! Listen toward life!*

> "Many people are looking for an ear that will listen . . . but the one who can no longer listen to one's brother or sister will soon be no longer listening to God either," Dietrich Bonhoeffer wrote in *Life Together.*

Religious people who load their speech with moralistic clichés might surprise themselves by trying out fresh metaphors, such as *turn* for "repent," *listen* for "obey," or *Love* for "God." Ironically, supposedly secular people yearn for meaningful spiritual language; words such as *soul, contemplation, forgiveness,* and *spiritual* are popular again—indicating a suffocated longing beneath the stale crust of moralistic religion.

The French mystic activist and philosopher Simone Weil wrote how "Christ came and took possession of me," while reading George Herbert's poem "Love bade me welcome." Agnostic at the time, she then spent her short life paying attention to God's presence in marginalized people—picking grapes, working in a Renault factory, and writing out of her experiences. "Purity," she wrote, "is the ability to contemplate defilement." After Weil's death, the French government issued a postage stamp bearing Weil's words: *Attention is the only faculty of the soul that gives us access to God.*

Turn. Pay attention. Notice a friend's countenance, your lover's tone of voice, your kids' clothes, a colleague's words, faces in magazine ads, people of color in a photo, your own eyes in the mirror. Just by noticing a strange feeling one morning, a man recalled a fragment of a scary dream about his leg. He called his physician. At 4:00 P.M. that day he had surgery for cancer in his thigh.

Many seekers have only fragments of forgotten religious language. *Dogma* is a surreal movie, and Creed is a rock group! Not knowing scriptures, catechisms, and creeds saddens your faithful elders. Yet losing religious words can be an advantage, because churchspeak is often an obstacle to lively faith.

Seekers are our teachers. Like the youthful Jesus teaching elders in the temple, like a dream of a precocious child, you call us back to innocent truth. Divested of shopworn *shibboleths,* youths and elders can explore new metaphors and media to communicate the truth of love.

A young adult recently called me to ask which translation of the Bible to get; he hadn't read it since fifth grade. I suggested some contemporary versions, especially *The Message* by Eugene Peterson.

But the current wave of translations hardly goes the distance. We need coaches who translate the ancient words into the vulgate of our own lives, where the word becomes vulnerable and vulgar again—carnal, in your flesh, in your face.

For example, "Are you redeemed?" sounds like such a pious question. But what if you look at the word *redeem* carefully? What if some wasted chapter of your own life, or that of another, can be re-deemed, re-valued?

A lot of secular people are not sure they know how to pray—and a lot of religious people are sure they do know how. For both, I offer a fresh working hypothesis from Evelyn Underhill, in *The Spiritual Life:* "Prayer means turning to Reality." *Turning to One Another: Simple Conversations to Restore Hope to the Future,* Margaret Wheatley's popular book reflecting on terrorist times, makes precisely this urgent plea: turn to the raw reality of the world and, with tenderness, to each other.

> You can contemplate the beauty of a rosebud or the pain of a car crash. Prayer is paying loving attention to the world's gore and splendor.

Turn and notice what is *real* in the places and people that dazzle or disturb you. This is where you encounter the Christ beneath Christianity, the Buddha way beneath the Buddha's words—in the least of these, on the edges, at the bottoms of things.

Reflection Exercise 7. Beginning Contemplative Prayer

Turn and notice what is *real* in the places that dazzle or disturb you. Simply become aware of these two extremes—in a moment of sitting, walking, driving, or going about daily activities. The places that get our attention often become our "prayer." At the beginning or ending of the day, spend a few minutes with no agenda, and notice what lures you or distracts you. What is life saying? Make some notes in your journal. Converse with a friend, or share with a group.

Reflection Exercise 8. Let a Text Draw You to "Here"

Quietly ponder a scripture verse from the Bible or another sacred text. Or try using "Here I am" (*hineni* in Hebrew), a human prayer response of Moses, Abraham, Isaiah, and Mary. Spend a few minutes simply repeating the text: "Here I am...." or *hineni*. Imagine being present to yourself . . . to your surroundings . . . to the Spirit . . . the Spirit being present to you. . . . Reflect, using your journal. (See also Resource Two at the end of this book.)

5

YEARNING YOUR WAY HOME

Holy Worldly Paths

Philosophy is really homesickness;
it is the urge to be at home everywhere.
—German poet Novalis

[Andy Warhol] helped change our idea of what art is and
what it can do. He made it look trashy and valuable, passive
and active, like nothing and like something.
—Holland Cotter, New York Times, July 14, 2002

Everyone is homesick. We journey away from some primal
Garden of Eden as we first begin to lose cherished experiences, weaning from a mother's breast, a childhood
friend's moving, betrayal by a parent or parent figure. "It is an
illusion that youth are happy, an illusion of those who have lost
it," wrote Somerset Maugham. Awareness of brokenness starts
way before one's thirties, as used to be assumed.

A common fairytale theme voices our fears and fantasies: a
child grows up orphaned on the street or abandoned to survive
in the animal world. Then through tragic circumstances and surprise, the child discovers she or he is really the offspring of
royalty.

> Many children grieve a fantasy family they never knew, watching the crazy Simpsons or reruns of the Waltons or the Brady Bunch.

In the moment of hearing such a story, we experience a hint of some primal bliss. Blaise Pascal wrote: "All these examples of wretchedness prove the human being's greatness. It is the wretchedness of a great lord, the wretchedness of a deposed king." Each of us yearns for the orphaned treasure of our true self.

HOLY WORLDLINESS: TWO PARADOXICAL PATHS HOME

To get back home, we try the path of self-pleasure or self-denial, or both together. Since ancient times, body piercing has represented a painful yearning for royal identity. Precious metals poke through our skin, announcing: "Something in me is precious!" Tattoos prick the body to create a mark of permanence on this swiftly tilting planet.

Secular and *spiritual* pop up as antonyms on my computer's thesaurus. But these two came together as I stood with friends in Pittsburgh's Andy Warhol museum, viewing Warhol's secular spiritual art. His paintings of Jesus at the Last Supper, framed with Campbell's soup, G.E., and cigarette logos, made *us* feel trashy and treasured, silly and serious, like something and like nothing, to adapt Holland Cotter's images. Traditions of East and West endorse both these seemingly opposite paths for coming home to your true self and the truth of love in a shattered cosmos.

In Hindu tradition, the paradox is similar to "the path of desire" and "the path of renunciation." We might also call them "the worldly path" and "the ascetic path." Like breathing in, the one speaks of *feasting* on life's good gifts; the other speaks of breathing out, emptying, *fasting* from things.

The first is the way of involvement and moves *toward* the world, using words and sensual images to draw one to the

sacred—the *via positiva,* or affirming way. The second is the way
of withdrawal, *away* from the world and images, finding the
sacred in silence, without words—the *via negativa,* or negating
way. "There is a time to keep silence, and a time to speak," says
the wise Hebrew sage in Ecclesiastes.

Luke, a physician interested in wholeness, shows us how
these two paths—fasting and feasting—are actually "cousins,"
like John the Baptist and Jesus. Luke brings together the
"ascetic way" of John the Baptist with the "worldly way" of
Jesus as the "Child of Humanity." John is rejected for being too
ascetic—in contrast to Jesus, who angers people for enjoying
life too much: "For John the Baptist has come eating no bread
and drinking no wine, and you say, 'He has a demon'; the Child
of Humanity has come eating and drinking, and you say, 'Look,
a glutton and a drunkard, a friend of tax collectors and sin-
ners!' "

Thus the Bible's image of wild John the Baptist in grunge
clothing makes sense: "Now John wore clothing of camel's hair
with a leather belt around his waist"—the ascetic path. Many
took offense at Jesus' worldlier path of eating, drinking, and
partying.

One big reason Jesus was rejected is clear: he was simply
having too much fun with the wrong kind of folks. In Luke's
Gospel, Jesus is on his way to a party, returning from one, getting himself invited to another, or telling stories about partying—mostly with the "little people," the *anawim* in Hebrew.
Add to this Jesus' radical claim that by including these outsiders
he was faithful to tradition while challenging party-line purity
codes, and it is politically explosive. The masses heard him
gladly, and that threatened the Romans.

So the cross is the final intertwining of the worldly and
the ascetic path, yielding to suffering for having claimed too
much joy for people on life's margins. The cross represents the
integrated life: doubting ("My God, why . . . ?") and believing
("I commit my spirit"), emptiness ("I thirst") and fullness ("It is

finished"), dying and rising. The spiritual life is a rhythm of turning away from the world to turn toward the world again.

DOUBTING BELIEVING IN MANY TRADITIONS

One can see the worldly path reflected in the lavish pantheon of Hindu gods—one for every need or desire. Contrast the Buddha's ascetic path, refusing to describe God at all: to define love would destroy love. This is why Buddhism is sometimes called an atheistic religion. Hence the phrase, "If you meet the Buddha, kill him" meaning, if you ever find yourself *possessing* enlightenment, kill the temptation to cling even to a good idea or experience. Do not mistake the finger that points to the moon for the moon.

We find the two paths in Judaism's kabala tradition: the *yesh* (there is) and the *ayn* (there is not). Mysteriously, like the lights and darks of chiaroscuro in Rembrandt's paintings, or the massive white space with spare lines of Japanese calligraphy, the two are interconnected. There is also the Jewish expression *yesh mit ayn*—something out of nothing. In the letter to the Hebrews, we read: "Things seen were made of things unseen."

> Our language about God points us to the place on the horizon beyond which is God.

Believers still sing "Immortal, invisible, God only wise, / in light inaccessible, hid from our eyes." In a hot desert, direct light destroys. Sometimes I just need to hide out in the shadow.

TWO PATHS INTERTWINED: THE WAY OF DOUBT, THE WAY OF FAITH

"My thoughts are not your thoughts," says God through Isaiah. Forget ideas about God. "God is no-thing," said Meister Eckhart. Shedding outworn certitudes can prepare us for the many-colored coat of new believing.

Can a believer without *any* doubts really believe? "I believe, help my unbelief!" a father in Mark's Gospel cries out to Jesus, on behalf of his son. At the end of Matthew's gospel, Jesus' disciples gather on a mountain to hear his final commission to go into all the world with the good news. We read, "they worshipped him; but some doubted."

Thomas Merton, a Trappist monk immersed in East and West, felt called to search the depths of faith in its silence, ambiguity, and certainty lying deeper than the bottom of anxiety. Merton speaks of a place with no easy answers, no pat solutions: "It is a kind of submarine life in which faith sometimes mysteriously takes on the aspect of doubt, when, in fact, one has to doubt and reject conventional and superstitious surrogates that have taken the place of faith. On this level, the division between Believer and Unbeliever ceases to be so crystal clear. It is not that some are all right and others are all wrong: *all* are bound to seek in honest perplexity. Everybody is an Unbeliever more or less!"

All spiritual reformers began by doubting their tradition in order to believe it more deeply. "Doubt is the ants in the pants of faith; it keeps us moving," writes Frederick Buechner in *Wishful Thinking.* Each of us is a paradox of questing and trusting—atheists, agnostics, and "true" believers. In his *Letters to a Young Poet,* Rainer Maria Rilke bids patience and love for the heart's unresolved questions: "Do not now seek the answers, which cannot be given you because you would not be able to live them. And the point is, to live everything. Live the questions now. Perhaps you will then gradually, without noticing it, live along some distant day into the answer."

Christ "emptied" himself (*kenosis* in Greek)—even though he was equal to God, according to Paul. "Christ was in the world *incognito*—unrecognized—and that was his *kenosis*"; so wrote Russian philosopher Nicholas Berdyaev, urging believers not to look down on doubters, even atheists. Rather, they should enter into their struggles and trials like Christ, *incognito*—without needing recognition—from below, without

> Our times of deprivation and doubt can be likened to a spiritual "fast" from the "feast" of believing and religious talk: "There is a time to break down, and a time to build up," says Ecclesiastes.

answers. So we need to shed many of our comfortable habits of thinking and living to identify with masses of the world's people.

Right when you feel like "nothing but a flimsy web of questions," to use poet Denise Levertov's phrase, you are handed the questions of others. Their questions may be answers woven mysteriously into your own journey home. Instead of avoiding the impasse, by staying with it, even finding a gift in it, a deeper faith is born.

STAGES ALONG LIFE'S WAY

There are lots of devious ways to avoid the impasse. I can deny my doubts and mask my questioning, hell-bent on *looking* good. Other times I am the playboy, placating my doubts with toys, success, or substances, hell-bent on *feeling* good. Sometimes I am the moralist; I stuff my questions prematurely with good works, hell-bent on *doing* good unto others whether they want good done unto them or not. Then too, I can get downright cynical, wallowing in anger at myself and everyone else, *not caring* what is good.

These can all be addictive. But this is the good news: any of these ways can become an authentic spiritual path to come home to oneself and God: play or pain, denial or guilt, cynicism or anger, good works or burnout.

Søren Kierkegaard, that maverick Dane who wrote "polite" books such as *Attack on Christendom,* described these as four "stages along life's way." I paraphrase them as *having fun, doing good, burning out,* and *coming home.* I have diagrammed them here as being cyclical rather than sequential, in the form of the sign for infinity.

Stages Along Life's Way

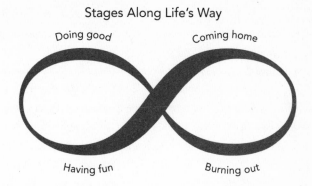

Doing good   Coming home

Having fun   Burning out

We see these movements in Jesus' parable of the "Prodigal" son who asks his dad for his inheritance and goes out and spends it all *having fun*. When he was empty, poor, and hungry, "he came to himself"—the first step in *returning home* to Love. The "Perfectionist" son stayed home *doing good*—but then exploded in resentment and rage. Each reached the stage of *burning out*, one by too much feasting on the world's pleasures, the other by too much righteous fasting from its pleasures.

Maybe you feel like the student who once said to me, "I think there is some of both the prodigal and the perfectionist in me." The world breaks everyone by one path or the other—too much fun or too much duty—or a paradox of both.

Some seem born into one path or the other, some from homes with strict rules, others from homes with no rules, one sibling going one way, another the opposite way. How is it that some seem to become strong at the broken places, and others do not?

Here is the best clue I know: at some blessed point, we may begin to see traces of grace right in the brokenness itself. To come to your self and your deepest desire is to come home to God.

My younger daughter's long struggles with anorexia, with late-night calls and desperate e-mails, caused me to take a personal inventory. My bankruptcy in fixing things led me to embrace my own deepest yearnings, fears, and hopes. I began to realize the demon of my own perfectionism was feeding into trying to measure up in the family system.

I realized I too was addicted—to looking good. Then I began to discover the joy of being freed from the burden of trying to be a good example, freed to experience the joy of being a *genuine* example. The move to a genuine example meant I would share my own insecurities, and the bond between us became closer. I recall one of her counselors telling me, "Spill coffee on yourself, often." That day I came home again to my vulnerable self.

My daughter began to come home to herself in a faraway part of the country. After years of struggle, during an in-patient treatment program, another patient's family became our daughter's home away from home, for three periods of time. On her last return, while living with her second family, she met a guy who likes to cook. He is now her lifelong lover and husband.

Pay attention to the stage you are in. Listen to your life. Be present to the pleasure, or the perfectionism, or the burnout; then you may find your true home. Kierkegaard understood what Martin Luther meant by "the strange work of love." Sometimes we have to follow love more deeply out on the edges of the world, and even get hurt, to find love at the center, "the proper work of love."

Love has to act strangely before it learns to act lovely. Then it acts strangely again, drawing us to a messiah hidden in people on the edges of life *and* in the marginalized parts of one's own soul. Now it is time to trek to the edge of thinking as an impasse—and, strangely, as a bridge to a new level of faith.

Reflection Exercise 9. Kierkegaard's "Stages Along Life's Way"

Meditate on Kierkegaard's "stages along life's way" (as I paraphrase them, and as diagrammed in this chapter): having fun, doing good, burning out, and coming home. Contemplate how they relate to the chapters of your own life journey. Are there times when you have been deeply into one or another? When you have cycled back and forth? Where would you assess that you are now?

Reflection Exercise 10. Beginning Centering Prayer

Meditate on your real desire; slow down your breathing. Allow a simple word to arise, one that seems to sum up that deep longing (examples are Love, Peace, Trust, One), or a short phrase of scripture such as "Be still, and know . . ." (Psalm 46:10)—or just *Be*. For some, a word in another language helps avoid thinking: *Amor* (love); *Shalom* or *Salaam* (peace in Hebrew and Arabic); *Maranatha* (Our Lord come, in Aramaic). Or a visual image or metaphor may arise. Begin repeating it, gently, in rhythm with your breathing . . . or visualizing it. . . . Then let go of the word or image, simply allow yourself to be present, loving, and being loved. (Try using this method to cultivate fifteen to twenty minutes of silence daily.) Log reflections in your journal.

6

THINKING YOUR WAY HOME

Postmodern Clues for
Primodern Faith

Truth is truth, whether from the lips of Jesus or Balaam.
—GEORGE MCDONALD

I thought I would feel guilty, but I didn't feel guilty at all.
What I felt was lonely.
—PETER, IN JOHN CHEEVER'S "A BOY IN ROME"

How can people love God and kill each other? How can seekers find truth if it is splintered into so many conflicting factions? The big barrier to thoughtful people is when believers' deeds contradict their creeds. It is a theological oxymoron.

If the messiah hides out in the marginalized, then Christ has been "crucified again and again" with a host of "heretics"— executed by fellow believers, martyred by outsiders, for believing differently, believing too much, believing too little—Jan Hus, Sir Thomas More, Ann Hutchinson, Gandhi, Martin Luther King Jr., Matthew Shepherd.

PRIMODERN FAITH: PRIMAL AND MODERN

I am calling for a new kind of faith: *passionate yet inclusive.* I choose to call this new kind of faith "primodern" because it seeks to unite our primal yearnings with modern learnings. Four cultural mind-sets can help to understand religious violence, and offer postmodern clues to help generate this kind of primodern faith.

PRIMAL ORAL MIND-SET

In the primal oral mind-set, faith is still passed down primarily through stories and music, rituals and gestures, memorizable proverbs or koans. One still encounters oral culture today in third-world countries, as well as in rural regions and villages and ethnic city areas of so-called developed countries. Oral communities form a rather closed loop; however, this culture has many correlations to modern pop culture, as I will describe in the emerging primodern culture.

LITERAL FUNDAMENTALIST MIND-SET

"Tradition is the living faith of the dead, but traditional*ism* is the dead faith of the living," runs an old proverb. Rigid belief systems, whether in religious or secular guise, freeze their founder's original ideas. A little doctrine set in stone is a dangerous thing; *-isms* paralyze the soul. Fundamentalism ignites hate and turns thinking people away from faith; still, in an anxious age people are drawn to it. However, fundamentals are good if used as foundation stones for building, not rocks for hurling.

MODERN RATIONAL MIND-SET

The Enlightenment era spawned individual creativity, analytical thinking, and democratic ideals. Yet for all its benefits, rationalism displaced the mythical and mystical. Theological education has been heavy on the *logical* and light on the *theo;* I did not have a single course on prayer or spiritual life in five years at two seminaries.

Nevertheless, I value modern critical scientific and literary tools; they help me take an intellectually honest look at sources of faith. For example, I value the work of the popular "Jesus seminar": What did Jesus *really* say and do? Picking up on Albert Schweitzer's classic *The Quest of the Historical Jesus,* Marcus Borg, John Dominic Crossan, and company opened up this nineteenth-century quest for twenty-first-century seekers. But after stripping away layers added by the early Gospel editors, how do you make sense of the "trimmed down" Jesus of history—and move to the Christ of experience?

POSTMODERN MIND-SET

Enter postmodern thought, which can hold such opposites as critical thinking and faith experience in creative paradox. Brian Greene offers an example in his best-seller *The Elegant Universe: Superstrings, Hidden Dimensions, and the Quest for the Ultimate Theory.* Greene wants to communicate this amazing T.O.E. (Theory of Everything) for lay folks like me; a superstring resembles an infinitely thin rubberband. The basic principle of T.O.E. is "that everything at its most microscopic level consists of combinations of vibrating strands—string theory provides a single explanatory framework capable of encompassing all forces and all matter." T.O.E. can take seemingly contradictory theories— Newton's gravity, Einstein's $e = mc^2$, and Heisenberg's uncertainty principle—and tie them up in one big bundle. So too, postmodern thought espouses mystery, and each solution begs a new question. This is the upside of postmodernism.

But its downside is loneliness and fragmentation. If everything is relative, without absolute truth, it becomes hard to develop community without having commonly accepted beliefs. The question Pilate asked Jesus at his trial sounds a bit postmodern, even cynical: "What is truth?" Jesus was silent. The world still waits. What if Pilate's unanswered question is the cry of each generation to discover truth in their own experience? This could forge a new kind of community, where each blind person gains respect for the others' descriptions of the elephant.

PRIMODERN: HIGH-TECH, HIGH-TOUCH

Postmodern sounds as if we have somehow moved beyond modernity and reason. Really? Are you reading this book? Do you use a computer? This is why I am putting forth a new term *primodern* with its goal to integrate our primal yearnings with modern learnings.

Primal culture has many similarities to modern tech culture. Sound-bite communications, like ancient riddles and parables, work well for many of us with ADHD (attention deficit hyperactive disorder) or dyslexic tendencies. Primal symbols and story, gestures and art, sports and music bridge all generations.

Primodern culture can wed the most advanced theories of science or politics or meaning with the innocent wonder of a child. Overlay a PowerPoint presentation of the Grand Canyon's geologic history with Yo-Yo Ma's cello and Bobby McFerrin's vocals (on the CD *Hush*); you have an immediacy of experience for today's tech set *and* their nonagenarian elders with short-term memory loss.

Primodern baptizes modern and primal: high-tech, high-touch. In *Quantum Spirituality,* Leonard Sweet writes that "the primal scream of postmodern spirituality is for primal experiences of God." That deep hunger, the Gallup Poll asserts, is the most important finding since its founding in 1935. Cool computer screens and impersonal institutions leave tech generations starved for spiritual intimacy in authentic community.

FROM DEMYTHING TO REMYTHING: CREATION AND SCIENCE

Three aspects of primodern culture can help our doubting believing quest. First, instead of demything miracle stories and fairy tales as silly, we can remyth them, connecting ancient poetic truth with our own broken narratives. Second, primoderns can

> Gesture, music, art, and poetry are the educated person's primal language, the reservoir of dreaming and daring, grieving and hoping.

return to primal language like "down" and "up" as metaphor, letting the immediacy of experience stand side by side with rational facts and ideas. Third, instead of simplistic either-or categories that divide people, paradox and process can hold differences in both-and creative tension.

For example, reclaiming poetic meanings can open dialogue with controversial "creation" scientists, who try to use science to argue a literalist reading of the six days of creation (Genesis 1). Modern rationalists point to hard "facts": The sequence of the "days" does not square with geological and anthropological time periods; snakes cannot talk; God did not walk in a garden in the evening; and Noah's flood, if it occurred at all, was quite local. And in the second creation story (Genesis 2), a day is not literal: the entire process is described as "the *day* that the Lord made the earth and the heavens...."

Yet both rationalists and literalists can agree that scientific research tries to tell us *how* creation evolves, whereas the Bible is telling us *why* we were created. Lots of books and sermons simply stop there: you do your thing; we'll do ours.

To explore the *why* of creation, primoderns could be quite happy producing a dramatic musical where snakes talk, God walks with Eve and Adam, and floods come for Mr. and Ms. Noah. All the characters, though, would be poetically related to the context of the listeners—one way in Kenya, another in Tokyo or New York.

Ancient characters would poke fun at contemporary issues, subtly using primal myth to tweak trite clichés of science, religion, and politics. Andrew Lloyd Webber's versions of "Joseph and the Amazing Technicolor Dreamcoat" and "Jesus Christ Superstar" are examples. Everybody from fundamentalist to atheist gets the meaning.

In an article called "The Evolution of Creation," Beth Rohrbach Perry, a minister and writer in Pennsylvania, offers diverse biblical images to describe the Creator in the process of creation: construction worker, baker, midwife, seamstress, mother, and father: "God measures, pounds, dyes, stores, begets and births to establish creation." Such metaphors from our ancestors can leave a scientist open to looking at data differently, and keep a believer from condemning the next Galileo.

"UP AND DOWN": EVEREST AND A "SECOND NAÏVETÉ"

Bishop John Shelby Spong tells how the late Carl Sagan humorously "proved" that Jesus could not have "ascended to heaven" in scientific terms. Given two thousand years, by Sagan's calculations, Jesus would still be zooming through a nearby galaxy! The ascension "myth" therefore seems to be left over from ancients who pictured God as up in the heavens, more accessible on mountaintops and in thunder and lightning. Moderns, knowing all about travel in outer space, cannot stomach such ideas as facts. Where is up? Or down?

Still, we primoderns go right on using the language of up and down. This is what Paul Ricoeur meant by a "second naïveté." We return to childhood terms but use them poetically, not literally. The computer is down. Downsizing a corporation does not mean shrinking its building or the person fired. As I walk my dog, I find myself singing lines of an African American spiritual: "Sometimes I'm up, sometimes I'm down . . . Sometimes I'm almost to the ground, O yes Lord." For many, like me, who live with bipolar disorder, music and ritual help us bless the wild rhythms of life (see Chapter Nineteen).

Modernity tried to steal our myths. We smile at primal peoples who still think God is closer on a mountain. But why do sophisticated Americans go trekking to retreat centers in the Catskills of upstate New York? An IMAX movie exhibits the

> We can be rational and primal. In the popular *Star Wars* movie series, a Jedi can defect to the dark side, Obi-Wan Kenobi is a prophet, and Anakin is born of a virgin. Primodern climate repoeticizes and remythologizes.

climber's lure for Mt. Everest, not unlike Moses' terrifying encounter with God on Mt. Sinai. "Mountaintop experience" is today's vocabulary for the ancient *mysterium tremendum*. The tremendous mystery that saves Everest's climbers is daring courage *and* holy fear. If you ever lose the fear, you are dead. Maybe we are all more primal than we think.

PRIMODERN: GROWN-UP *AND* CHILDLIKE

When I was young, my mother once confided in me that my grandmother Mame thought "the sun rose and set on Woodrow Wilson"—a Democrat in my Republican family! I knew exactly what the expression meant, though I also knew the sun is actually a star, and it is the earth that moves so the sun does not rise or set. Nor had President Wilson gotten sunburned in its rays.

What is the difference between personifying God ("The sound of the Lord God walking in the garden in the cool of the day")—and the stock market ("Wall Street got nervous at the sound of saber rattling")? A reporter tells us that "oil" has enough votes for drilling Alaskan reserves, and we understand that indigenous people's pleas to save the caribou do not have a chance. Wall Street's sidewalks do not have nerve endings; my car's oil does not vote. Metaphors allow us to be grown-up and childlike at the same time.

I tell my newly discovered New England cousin that I will "walk" with him through a major vocational transition, but I do not mean I will develop huge legs that straddle all the way from Pennsylvania to New Hampshire. In the same way I can say God has walked with me through many dangers, toils, and snares. It is a very personal walk, but God does not need feet and toes. But as I write this, listening to the African American singing group Sweet Honey in the Rock, my feet and toes echo a rhythm out of heaven—and Incarnation happens. *Walk* embodies Paul Ricoeur's second naïveté: my *personal* walk with God, and my *ethical* life in the world: "Walk the talk."

FACTS AND TRUTH: PARADOX AND PROCESS

A monk who had lived in Rwanda told me of a decades-old dispute between two groups. When a new chief called a council, a man stood up and began "putting the facts straight," though he was rehearsing the same old grievances—dates, names, specific atrocities. The chief interrupted: "We're not here to restate the facts, but to find a solution that embodies a truth we can all live with."

Metaphor and story weave truths with facts. A young woman got help for her quest from Japanese novelist Shusako Endo's *A Life of Jesus.* Endo distinguishes between truth and fact. The timeless truth of the gospel—that Love bounces back—can absorb the wildest scholarly guesses about the facts of Jesus' empty tomb.

Primoderns can simultaneously question the facts of a tradition and still appreciate the truth it bears. T. S. Eliot muses on this tension: "The hint half guessed, the gift half understood, is Incarnation."

Paradox embraces this doubting believing tension. Characters in a story, movements in a dance, moods in a symphony, surreal animals in mythical lands give voice to mysterious buried energies in all of us.

In C. S. Lewis's series *The Chronicles of Narnia,* children on a rainy afternoon in England push the coats back in a wardrobe—and it opens to the imaginary icy land of Narnia, "where it is always winter but never Christmas." There they encounter Aslan the Lion, who embodies the mythical paradox of gentle compassion and fierce strength—a Christ figure. The children have to leave home to find home in a strange country.

> Here is primodern leadership: you realize experience skews the facts; therefore pursuing truth is a process of finding life-giving goals while living with unresolved points of view.

Incarnation still happens. The mythical Aslan comes alive in real time and space, in the form of a "family" of Canadians who transform the cold prison system of the United States. *The Hurricane* is the true film story of Rubin "Hurricane" Carter, who was wrongfully imprisoned for murder in Patterson, New Jersey. Against great odds, Carter writes his autobiography from prison but gives up on ever being released. Years later an alienated American youth, Lesra, now living in Canada, finds his life changed by Carter's story. Lesra starts corresponding with Carter in prison.

Finally, Lesra convinces his three adult guardians to leave their beautiful Canadian home and move down to a Jersey high-rise across from where Carter is confined on death row. They choose to leave home to find home. They advocate for Hurricane, even when he no longer believes in himself, even when he rejects their help, even when self-styled militarists stalk them and threaten their sanity. The family's human belief in Hurricane functions like an icon of God believing him into new life. Their "hint half guessed, the gift half understood, is Incarnation." The Word still becomes flesh.

Here is a living specimen of human love permeating profane systems. We would do better to half-guess and half-understand than to think we are so right that we kill off people or ideas. It might change our view of capital punishment—and capital investment. To recast Luther, *Doubt boldly; love more boldly still.*

A PRIMODERN LENS

In John Cheever's story "A Boy in Rome," Peter decides to play hooky from school and gets a job as a guide for a tour company named Roncari. Peter comes home nights, pretending to his mother that he is going out to school each morning. Then he reveals what was happening inside himself: "I thought I would feel guilty, but I didn't feel guilty at all. What I felt was lonely."

A boy in Rome is *us*. With absolutes, even false truths, we used to know when to feel guilty or make others guilty and kill them. In a postmodern era that lacks clear rights and wrongs, we think up new ways to demonize others and inflict them with bombs and bullets, by imprisoning them or pretending they are invisible.

But we have been trained not to admit guilt. So we stave off incredible loneliness by helplessly inflicting pain on our own bodies, with too much food or lack of food, with drugs or death. Or we stuff the loneliness by adding on: relationships, careers, toys, technology, real estate, even religion. Fill the vacuum. More is better.

Instead, what if we begin to embrace the loneliness by listening to our bodies? That would be primodern. As one young adult said to me, "I need to honor my reptilian self." Spiritual awareness means honoring the ancient animal aspects in each of us. Our bodies' groans and grunts are a signal to our primal soul: *Wake up!*

Reflection Exercise 11. Your Own Light and Sound Show

Locate a small bell and ring it. Where is the sound? In the vibrations of the bell? in the sound waves? or in your ear drum? Enter a room on a sunny day. Stretch out your hand to where the sun is beaming through an open door or window. Where is the sun? Is it ninety-three million miles away? dancing in a beam of dust particles? or on your hand?

Ponder the mysteries of sound, how words are only vibrations. We could translate the first words in the Bible as "And God vibrated (or sounded), 'Let there be light.'" In spiritual traditions, light is a metaphor for God, and God is love; how is love like light? (For more insight about light, go online or use an encyclopedia.) Reflect on this experience with someone.

7

SWEATING YOUR WAY HOME

Body Language

The body is truly the garment of the soul, which has a
living voice. . . .
—HILDEGARD OF BINGEN, ELEVENTH-CENTURY MYSTIC AND MUSICIAN

The body takes the shape of the soul.
—ANONYMOUS MYSTIC

"You play the bass like it is part of your body."
—A FRIEND'S COMMENT TO TOM BEAUDOIN

Tobin's term paper held my attention as he reflected on an
encounter with God during a cross-cultural trip doing
construction work: "Sweating My Way Home," he called
it. Some personality types tend to think their way home—like
C. S. Lewis. Others like Tobin are more prone to sweat their way
home. Body language is their primary speech.

Tom Beaudoin writes in *Virtual Faith:* "My experiences
playing rock were usually more religious than I had found in
most churches . . . traversing the deep rhythm, riding the low
notes, or stomping through a syncopated rumble, *something happens.*" Beaudoin tells how a woman said, "You play the bass like

In France, peasant workers would use an expression if an apprentice got tired or injured: "It's the trade entering his body."

it is part of your body." He calls it "rock religiosity."

THE BODY SOUL SPLIT

One of the big barriers to spirituality is the equation of the body versus soul split into bad versus good. Despite exceptions to the contrary, ascetic disciplines are meant to enhance the whole person, including the body, not to degrade it.

In Jewish-Christian tradition, the idea of resurrection of the body is a bold affirmation that new life in the Spirit blesses the whole human person, right here in this world. The apostle Paul insists the body is a "temple of the Holy Spirit." Likewise Basava, a twelfth-century Hindu reformer, reflects on the body as a sacred temple:

> The rich will make temples for Siva:
> What shall I, a poor man, do?
> My legs are pillars, the body is a shrine,
> The head is the cupola, of gold.

Could it be that if we really listened to these temple-bodies we might hear the echoes of the lost liturgies of our lives?

THE BODY TAKES THE SHAPE OF THE SOUL

Etched in my mind is the hunched figure of a six-foot-six professional and scholar, silhouetted in a hallway in late afternoon sun. I thought of the ancient wisdom, "The body takes the shape of the soul." Exchanging greetings, he entered my office.

We sat for a bit in silence. I sensed his discouragement. Soon he drifted into talking about tiredness, the value of "shutting down the computers"—of being instead of doing. At some point I found myself asking, "What is sabbath for you?"

"Well, reading," he said, "but I haven't been reading much. Taking my boat on the river, but I don't take time. Walking with my wife, but I get home late at night. And music."

"Oh?" I queried.

"A bit of piano. And the trumpet—I used to play with my family, but my lip isn't even in shape anymore."

A year and many experiences later, this gentleman received an award from his alma mater for excellence in his profession. The night of the awards banquet, he was standing tall. Afterward I met his wife, who began telling me how one evening she had come home from teaching in a nearby college. "And when I heard the trumpet, I knew something was changing in my husband."

Howard Gardner's work on multiple intelligences offers a holistic lens for restoring body and soul in all of life. Some intelligences are highly developed in a person, others less, yet everyone has some aptitude in each. I offer a brief spiritual spin here and refer to them throughout coming chapters.

- *Linguistic/verbal:* Just as a child cannot live isolated from speech, so a seeker needs a community of journeyers to develop the language of mindfulness and love.
- *Logical/mathematical:* Theo-*logical* insight means reflecting on the experience of the sacred—faith seeking understanding and symbolic expression.
- *Spatial/visual:* Spatial learning arranges a room, explores geography, plans cross-cultural events, designs holy space, and creates fantasy.
- *Musical/rhythmic:* "One who sings prays twice." Singing, drumming, or piping your troubles makes the blues beautiful and celebrates life's rhythms.
- *Kinesthetic/bodily:* Gestures begin a symphony, decide a baseball game, and express the soul: bowing, kneeling, clapping, dancing, crafting, playing games.

- *Interpersonal:* Extroverts tend to encounter the Sacred in community, introverts in small groups or one-to-one; both need relationships.
- *Intrapersonal:* Most neglected in technological society, solitude is an introvert's joy and preserves the extrovert's sanity.
- *Naturalist:* The Sacred is revealed through the "book of nature"—its awe and beauty, its patterns of devastation and renewal.
- *Existentialist:* "Why are we here? Where are we going?" Philosophers and artists, mystics and poets voice everyone's questions about life's meaning.

For three centuries, René Descartes's maxim "I think, therefore I am" has skewed modern Western culture toward printed, logical, and technological intelligence. But if you examine only what you "think" you believe, you can end up feeling like a spiritual flunky. Actually, you may "know" the Holy in your experience, in your gut, your heart—your primal brain.

We need primal cultures' richness in the other areas, and vice versa. The primodern spiritual quest is to link our primal knowing with modern knowledge.

Creative storytelling is a way to participate in facets of all nine learning modes: witness stories told as operas, musicals, ballads, dances, and dramas. A Hassidic story tells of a *rebbe,* a respected Jewish teacher, who was crippled and bedfast for years. In struggling to light the first Hanukah candle, he began to tell how his grandfather used to sing and dance. As the old man was telling it, he hobbled on his twisted feet and began singing and dancing. That is how to tell a story. *The body takes the shape of the soul.*

THE SOUL TAKES THE SHAPE OF THE BODY

If you think about it, the opposite is also true: *the soul takes the shape of the body.* If the body is tense, as Herbert Benson demonstrated in his popular book *The Relaxation Response,* our physical, spiritual, and emotional health is at risk. The spiritual journey can begin (or begin again) by finding the gift in the grit of the body's aches and ecstasies, its abilities and disabilities. There is no such thing as disembodied spirituality.

One December morning, I lifted a tire the wrong way. After four months of excruciating pain, I found myself having back surgery on my thirty-second birthday. Then an amazing thing happened: thanks to the accident, I literally "backed" into a disciplined time of meditation and prayer. Prescribed exercises have become gestures of gratitude or prayers for others. I find that practicing tai chi and yoga stretches with breathing strengthens my body and opens the human spirit. Physical balancing encodes my psyche with inner balance.

If the body is uptight or upright, so is the soul. I have seen people in wheelchairs whose bodies mirror more self-esteem than able-bodied persons slouched at computers.

The film *Awakenings* dramatizes this kind of embodied spirituality. It is based on the true story of Dr. Oliver Sacks. The maverick young physician (played by Robin Williams) observes the stone faces of catatonic patients in a mental hospital. He has a hunch that somewhere beneath these death masks there lies a suffocated flame of life. Bucking the medical establishment, the doctor risks his career by using an experimental drug to liberate people perceived as the living dead.

Awakenings is a parable of how secular society's fast pace and institutional structures etherize our bodies and souls. Afraid to buck the system, we sell our souls to economic, educational, military, religious, and political schemes that deaden our creative spirit.

Down deep, we live with the gnawing truth that our expansive Western way of life and work depends on sweatshops, poverty, and hunger in poor and Southern hemisphere nations. Consequently we live only half-awake, and our bodies become more susceptible to toxins and cancers, creating physical, emotional, and spiritual paralysis.

When *Time* gave its 2002 "Persons of the Year" award to whistleblowers Cynthia Cooper of WorldCom, Coleen Rowley of the FBI, and Sherron Watkins of Enron, we breathed in a bit of their daring courage to expose the breakdown of corporate values.

KINESTHETIC SPIRITUALITY

Yearn your way home, think your way home or sweat your way home—breath, brains, or brawn. Spirit, mind, and body all become prayer. Any way you journey home means waking up.

Sometimes when you cannot feel or think your way back home, you just have to find a way to put your body in the grit.

> When Rabbi Abraham Heschel marched with Martin Luther King Jr. at Selma, he was quoted as saying, "I prayed with my legs as I walked." This is kinesthetic spirituality.

A proper Nantucket woman normally stayed as far as she could from church or pain or the sight of blood. But on the last night of a friend's life, acting on impulse, she lay down in her friend's bed and held her expiring body, breath by labored breath, into a peaceful death in morning's light. When the mind cannot think its way into feeling loved or loving, the body can take us on the journey back home to compassion.

This is not programming divine love or winning a spiritual merit badge. It is simply placing your whole self into the grit of life, where you become porous enough for the grace to seep in.

Reflection Exercise 12. Physical Exercise as Prayer

Reframe physical exercise as prayer: jogging, walking, or prescribed exercise for your back or body, yoga or tai chi practice. Begin with mindfulness and thankfulness . . . for air . . . light . . .

colors . . . breathing . . . nerve endings . . . brain cells . . . muscles.
. . . Consider motion as a prayer of thanks (arms uplifted) . . . or
of concern (hands cupped as if lifting a friend to the light). Or
try beginning your exercise routine with a line of a poem, a
verse of scripture, or a song that summons up your hope for the
day, meditating on it as you exercise, or walk, or run.

Reflection Exercise 13. Menial Jobs as Prayer

As you go about hard work, mow grass, take out garbage, clean
a toilet, or make a bed, engage in the task with mindfulness. . . .
Dedicate these times "with special intention" for fellow laborers, migrant workers, restaurant servers, housekeeping staff . . .
for any who earn a living doing manual labor. Option: Using
your journal, reflect on a past work experience or service project, being attentive to any edge of spiritual growth. Everything
becomes a prayer if you mean it so.

WONDER HAPPENS

Surprise! Surprise.

Concepts create idols; only wonder comprehends anything. People kill one another over idols. Wonder makes us fall on our knees.
—St. Gregory of Nyssa

For a transitory enchanted moment man must have held his breath. . . . face to face for the last time in history with something commensurate to his capacity for wonder.
—F. Scott Fitzgerald, The Great Gatsby

"But where shall I find courage?" asked Frodo. "That is what I chiefly need now." "Courage is found in unlikely places," said Gildor. "Be of good hope! Sleep now."
—J.R.R. Tolkien, The Lord of the Rings

8

DREAMS, DAYDREAMS, AND DISCOVERY

Resemblances and antitheses make of each resemblance a
reason for surprise in the next difference and of each difference a reason for surprise in the next resemblance.
—Gerard Manley Hopkins

Let things that would ordinarily bore you suddenly
thrill you.
—Andy Warhol

I was standing in a parking lot when the question came to me:
What would I believe if I didn't believe anything? The first
thing I *knew* deeper than traditional beliefs was that any bits of
insight or wonder emerge through the grit of life. The second
thing was that insight or wonder cannot be programmed; it happens by surprise. My mind was abuzz with myriad scientific,
political, athletic, and artistic examples.

Important discoveries are not born full-blown but in
"acorn" fashion, when a tiny experience breaks open unexpect-
edly in a person's life to create a greater purpose.

WONDER IN THE WORLDS OF SCIENCE, ARTS, AND POLITICS

After working in the chemistry lab to discover the molecular structure of benzene, a young professor came home for supper. Dozing afterward near a fireplace in 1859, Friedrich August Kekulé von Stradinitz dreamed of the ancient symbol of a serpent biting its tail. Kekulé feverishly gathered data validating his intuition, which is still the accepted theory of the Benzene ring. Regardless of the story's facts, it is true to the surprise nature of Kekulé's discovery.

While boarding a streetcar in Zurich, a self-taught student glanced at the town clock and instantly "knew" that $e = mc^2$. The acorn of Albert Einstein's whole career in miniature cracked open—from a kid who did poorly in school to a postal clerk to the most brilliant human being of his time.

On a leisurely Sunday afternoon's stroll across Glasgow Green, James Watt had a sudden insight on how to make an effective steam condenser.

Wislawa Szymborska, winner of the 1996 Nobel Prize for literature, writes of the faith it takes to say "I don't know": "Had my compatriot Marie Sklodowska-Curie never said to herself 'I don't know,' she probably would have wound up teaching chemistry at some private high school for young ladies from good families."

Mme. Curie could have easily chosen the security of the boarding school job. But she chose to follow the insecure path of *not* knowing, and because of that we experience the benefits of radium—her famed discovery with her husband, Pierre.

Surprise happens in the grit of archeological excavation. In the region of Ethiopia 140 miles northeast of the capital of Addis Ababa, Yohannes Haile-Selassie (no relation to the emperor), from the University of California, Berkeley, recently found what appears to be the most ancient human ancestor ever discovered. But Haile-Selassie was not specifically looking

Lazy students left poorly cleaned staphylococcus culture plates in an unheated lab. Noticing that a liquid mold culture had created a bacteria-free circle around itself, Alexander Fleming discovered penicillin—by accident and shrewd observation.

for the things he found. He had set out to better understand how ancient ecosystems worked; "I didn't even think about finding hominids," he says. Then in December 1997, at a place called Alayla, he spotted a piece of jawbone lying on the rock-strewn ground.

Wonder happens in the world of the arts. It was amateur night at the Harlem Opera House. A scrawny sixteen-year-old went on stage, ready to dance. She hesitated, and the announcer said: "The next contestant is Miss Ella Fitzgerald. . . . Hold it, hold it. Now what's your problem, honey? . . . Correction, folks. Miss Fitzgerald has changed her mind. She's not gonna dance, she's gonna sing. . . ." So she did, followed by three encores and first prize. In a moment the acorn of her call to sing, not dance, burst open.

It happens in the social, military, and political arenas. Such leaders as Abraham Lincoln, Mohandas Gandhi, Eleanor Roosevelt, and Martin Luther King Jr. seized the day against surprising odds. Jason, the young military leader I spoke of earlier, could not explain why the "enemy" forces walked away from his startled little band of Americans, whom they could have easily destroyed.

Surprise timing cracked open the world of sports. Wilma Rudolf, nicknamed "the black gazelle," overcame physical and racial barriers to win the Olympics. Jackie Robinson, with Branch Rickey's affirmation, broke the barrier of race, exploding into baseball's major leagues. In *The Tipping Point*, Malcolm Gladwell shows that hard work alone is not the key to such breakthroughs. It is the serendipity of timing and connections.

WHAT DO THESE AHAS TEACH US?

Whether theories of the galactic universe or of subatomic particles—or a grand Theory of Everything, as Brian Greene describes string theory in *The Elegant Universe*—discovery often comes through doing nothing, in a moment of *not* working on a problem.

These surprise discoveries, though born in acorn fashion, function like a hologram that contains some cosmic insight. First, they are preceded by rigorous and often boring work on the part of the discoverer. Then comes a crisis or an impasse—the moment of agnosticism, of doubting the current data yet knowing more deeply that there *is* something beyond the facts. This very futility, this letting go, this unknowing is the fertile seedbed for discovery. Difficulties frequently increase the nearer one approaches the goal.

Then the delight of discovery is followed by another period of work, observing subsequent manifestations that validate the "aha" of the original insight.

This fourfold pattern of intense ordinary working, a pause of not working, then an "Aha" followed again by working—has direct parallels in the spiritual life. It is echoed in a Zen teaching:

> What did you do before enlightenment?
> I chopped wood and I carried water.
> What do you do after enlightenment?
> I chop wood and I carry water.

In *Mystics and Zen Masters,* Thomas Merton quotes the fourteenth-century teacher Bassui, "You will perceive the Master only after you have probed 'What is it?' with your last ounce of strength and every thought of good and evil has vanished."

Annie Dillard describes this radical serendipity in *The Writing Life:* "The experience of writing is like any unmerited

When Gerard Manley Hopkins spoke of resemblances and antitheses creating a reason for surprise, he was making a point that the element of astonishment is wired into human experience.

grace. It will be handed to you, but only if you are looking for it. You search, you break your heart, your back, your brain, and then— and only then—it is handed to you."

But you can never tell when. Dillard writes: "One line falls from the ceiling . . . and you tap in the others around it with a jeweler's hammer . . . and wait suspended until the next one finds you."

So what does this have to do with spiritual practices? You dream, you talk, you walk, you pray, you work. But you do it all just to keep your eyes open. Then, when something magical breaks through the chaos, it arrives as "effortless effort" in the ordinary work of science, sports, art, music, mathematics—or relationships.

All you can do is prime the pump for some underground well of wonder to gush forth.

Then you chop wood and carry water again. Once in a long while, the wood catches fire that lights the universe, and the water be- comes an ocean of love.

Reflection Exercise 14. Cluster Journaling: Right Brain, Left Brain

Open yourself for surprise in relation to an issue where you need some clarity. In the center of a page, put down a word or image describing the concern; then create a cluster of thoughts around and below it, branching off like twigs of a tree, or like a spider web—writing or drawing with free-flow association, whatever images or thoughts occur to you (right brain). Then below all this, write a prayer, poem, or idea in sentences (left brain), picking up phrases or images you used in the cluster.

Reflection Exercise 15. Journal a Night Dream or a Day Dream

Dreams are a way to listen to our unconscious longings, warnings, and hopes; active imagination in daydreams has a similar effect. Everyone dreams, though some people do not recall them (largely because modern culture does not value dreams— "I had a silly dream last night"). Write out your dreams or draw them in your journal. At the end, write "Reflections" and leave space to make connections with practical issues and long-term decisions in your day-to-day life. Try using dream categories such as brakelights (warning), nightlights (reassurance), and headlights (invitation or vocation). Find a spiritual companion with whom to share dreams.

For more information on this practice, see Morton Kelsey, *Dreams: A Way to Listen to God* (New York: Paulist Press) and Robert Johnson, *Inner Work: Using Dreams and Active Imagination for Personal Growth* (San Francisco: HarperSanFrancisco).

9

SERENDIPITY!

Surprise Hunger for "Soul Talk"

God is right up there with sex!
—STEVE WALDMAN, COFOUNDER OF BELIEFNET.COM

oes just *any* surprise invention qualify as a *spiritual* experience, or only as a secular discovery to support a greedy culture's idea of progress? Is its discoverer transformed as a human being? What makes a so-called secular experience sacred? After all, $e = mc^2$ led to atomic devastation in Japan in 1945, and the dangers increase daily.

First, any experience of insight or creativity has the potential for constructive or destructive purposes. Second, I have offered these examples as *neutral* analogies of how truth sneaks up on us, unawares. The problem is, people have powerful experiences in their ordinary lives and work but are starving for a place to explore a spiritual and ethical connection.

SERENDIPITY: THE SECULAR CITY AND THE SURPRISE RETURN TO "SOUL TALK"

Dietrich Bonhoeffer, martyred for his protest against Hitler, issued a call for "religionless Christianity" in his *Letters and*

Papers from Prison. It was deeply rooted in a secular mystical combination: "prayer *and* righteous action" in the world.

Forty years ago, I read Bonhoeffer and vowed to join others to create cross-cultural exchanges and settle refugee families, protest capital punishment and work for peace, advocate for immigrants and work for just prison systems—and oppose religious bigotry. Many of us religious and secular folks have worked side by side to address poverty, tend the environment, and challenge political systems. Interfaith groups from Poughkeepsie to Pasadena organize soup kitchens and housing initiatives and job fairs.

But we forgot about prayer and burned out in the action. I've just dusted off my 1960s copy of *The Secular City,* where Harvey Cox said that religion's only value was secular involvement in the politics of social change. In the same period, Thomas Altizer and William Hamilton wrote books loudly proclaiming the earlier verdict of Friedrich Nietzsche: "God is dead!"

We can see the truth that the God of Western colonialism and male-biased triumphalism still needs to die. In the words of poet Adrienne Rich, "Something has to die in order for us to begin to know our truths. Perhaps we have to lose our national fantasies." But losing our national fantasies makes us hungry for spiritual reality.

"Today, it is secularity, not spirituality, that may be headed for extinction," Harvey Cox writes in *Fire from Heaven,* about the global rise of Pentecostal Christianity. He admits his *Secular City* missed the mark. So-called secular cultures are in fact a lot like India—a potpourri of spiritual hotbeds.

"God is right up there with sex!" said cofounder of Beliefnet.com Steve Waldman. Books abound with *soul* in the title: *Soul Mates, Soul Friend, SoulTsunami, Care of the Soul, Seat of the Soul, Time for My Soul, Chicken Soup for the Soul,* and *The Soul of Tomorrow's Church.* Spirituality is a hot topic; witness bulging bookstore shelves and links on the Internet.

The big surprise is that today's young adults are now seeking precisely what modern generations have lost: ancient practices to celebrate the Sacred, to transform individuals and institutions. However, this is not the 1950s and people are not flocking to houses of worship. We are believers in exile, as expressed in so many Hebrew "psalms of disorientation": "How could we sing the Lord's song in a foreign land?" Where can spiritual orphans turn?

> Surprise: when mainstream theology tried to avoid Godtalk, then pop culture resurrected words such as *soul* and *spirituality*.

SPIRITUAL EXPERIENCE WITH NOWHERE TO GO

A doctoral student at Lancaster Theological Seminary conducted research on "spiritual experiences," and many students and faculty (including me) participated. He found that even among theologically literate people, only a tiny minority had ever shared their experiences in a religious community or with a clergyperson.

To my chagrin, the student's finding resonates with an event from my own early ministry. A young adult came to me to tell of experiencing a spiritual "Presence." Later she confided to my wife that she felt I "dissed" her: I warned her not to let such things get out of hand. Had I known of the ancient art of spiritual direction, I could have explored with her how to integrate what was happening in a broadening perspective.

Every year around Christmas and Easter in *U.S. News & World Report, Time,* and *Newsweek,* pollsters report the same old story: large numbers of people have deep spiritual experiences, but they do not feel free to share them in religious communities.

LIVING AWAKE: WHY SPIRITUAL PRACTICES?

Disciples: How difficult is enlightenment?
Master: Oh, it is effortless, like the sunrise!
Disciples: Then why all these burdensome disciplines?
Master: Ah! So that you will be awake when the sun rises.

So Anthony de Mello's thoughts prod us in *The Song of the Bird:* What can we do to live awake? For more than three decades, I have been privileged to hear a rainbow of people's treasured epiphanies, and to read accounts of many others.

Transforming encounters happen in parking lots and cathedrals, in emergency rooms and classrooms, while stopped on a dangerous highway or transfixed by a sunrise.

They occur in crises or ordinary times, in solitude or community, to spiritual folks or secular folks. They can come as a practical insight to a problem, or as a purely mystical experience, occasionally in a religious celebration, more frequently in worldly activity.

But there is one consistent quality: *the element of surprise.* Such moments of wonder are never programmed. They just happen. Spiritual practices have no value except to help us to "be awake when the sun rises." Often a single experience forms a seamless union of mystical vision and political action—as in the next example.

SURPRISE WEDDING: THE MYSTICAL AND THE POLITICAL

As an ordinary schoolteacher in the 1970s, Julia Esquivel had no plans ever to be known as a political activist and feminist theologian. In personal conversation, she told me how she had begun to see disturbing mystical visions about her beloved

Guatemala, causing her much distress. When she began to express them in revolutionary poetry, the government silenced her, forcing her to live exiled in Europe. Now back in Guatemala, Esquivel exemplifies how embracing fear can in the same moment mean embracing faith, the union of mystical experience and risk-taking action, all by surprise.

So why do we not pay attention to such awe-full moments with more frequency? Two clues emerge toward an answer, each based on the same reason: *fear.* Some of us fear entering the void because the bliss we might discover is too close to some pain we have walled off just to survive. Or, like Julia Esquivel, we fear the risk and responsibility that would await us if we were to venture forth on such an awesome journey.

Either way, what if, as with good science, you were to follow these hypotheses, these educated hunches that might lead you home to your true self? What if, in the words of mythologist Joseph Campbell, you actually would "follow your bliss"— whether the frightening glory of Everest or the peaceful solitude of Walden Pond?

What if, in the words of Annie Dillard, you were to find your one thing necessary and "dangle from it limp, wherever it takes you"? What would it be like to take the leap of faith?

MARKS OF GENUINE SPIRITUAL EXPERIENCE

Hell in traditions of East and West is a life of boredom or dog-eat-dog aggression. As Yeats wrote, "The best lack all conviction, and the worst / are full of passionate intensity." Heaven is the opposite of apathy or hate.

You are invited to a risk-taking mission, the hint of a dream half-guessed, the gift half-understood. It is a twin mission of doubting *and* believing enough to risk being your true self, one so scary you might not attempt it if you understood it. In "Tintern Abbey," William Wordsworth writes, "And I have felt / A presence that disturbs me with the joy / Of elevated thoughts."

Two marks of genuine spiritual experience are that it both delights and disturbs. Wonder is *terrific* and *terrifying*. It causes you to feel lonely but it refuses to let you stay alone. Suspect any spirituality with too much *I* and *me* and not enough *us* and *we*. The English poet priest John Donne was right: "No one is an island entire of itself." A sense of community is another mark of genuine spiritual life.

But the ultimate mark of genuine versus counterfeit spiritual experience in all faith traditions is compassion. It can be summed up by Jesus: "By their fruits you shall know them." *Here is the acid test:* Does the experience bear the fruit of freedom to love?

I have taken some time to describe how genuine characteristics of wonder can arise out of suffering *or* success, in time of crisis or happiness. If fear is the obstacle to living awake, then any practices to release fear increase our freedom to love.

When we break free of boring patterns or places in our lives, no matter how minor, it can create the porous opening for an epiphany. Spiritual breakthroughs in little matters give us courage to take bigger risks. One sure way out of the bondage of hell is to let yourself be surprised.

Serendipity is the quality possessed by three island heroes in Henry Walpole's *The Three Princes of Serendip*. In popular use, serendipity is the art of making desirable discoveries by surprise. Spirituality is the art of discerning the *desirable* qualities in the process of life's discoveries.

How can we discern what is desirable as we face the human genome project? What is desirable on this swiftly tilting planet where the miracles of medical science are strangely skewed toward the wealthier Northern hemisphere?

The "Good News"—*Godspel* in Old English—breaks the spell of our boring compulsive cultural machines. Paying attention to moments of awe gives life direction and meaning.

Practice being awake when the sun rises. Something wants to be born.

Cradle Credo
Begin Life In
cradle: Be held.
Credo! Behold!
Return as a
child
to wonder
. . . again . . . and . . . again. . . .

Reflection Exercise 16. Surprise Yourself: Do Things the Opposite Way

Take a different route to work or school. . . . Put on the opposite sock first. . . . Zip your jacket with your left hand (or right hand if you are left-handed). . . . Eat a meal with the opposite hand. . . . Brush your teeth after having sex (or before, whichever breaks a pattern). Try some of these things for a week. Then reflect on the experiments. See if the simple physical experience opens up a new awareness of sensory observations or spiritual insight.

10
SHOCK.
9/11 and Traumatic Surprise

We have two or three great moving experiences in our
lives—experiences so great and so moving that it doesn't
seem at the time anyone else has been so caught up and
pounded and dazzled and astonished and beaten and broken
and rescued and illuminated and rewarded and humbled in
just that way ever before.
—F. Scott Fitzgerald

What happens to us when tragic events mark our lives
forever as before and after? What kind of God can
you believe in after a family suicide? after being
abused by your lover? after 9/11? What is there left to believe in
a world of violence and injustice?

"That kind of surprise I don't need," runs an old line. Surprise can take the form of energizing serendipity or paralyzing
shock: surprise! or surprise. Either can be the occasion that leads
to living dead or living awake. What makes the difference? The
tragedy of AIDS can devastate relationships. So can the hype of
winning the lottery.

I listened to Christopher Reeve speak as he used a ventilator and sat in a wheelchair. The turning point from despair to hope was his wife's words: "You're still you." The former Superman has found a passionate new vocation, working on behalf of others who suffer from critical injuries to the nervous system. He is living awake.

How can it be that even traumatic surprises contain some redeeming elements, some microchips of meaning to help us revalue the abandoned pieces of life?

SHOCK: WHAT HAPPENS IN TRAUMATIC SURPRISE?

What happens in the time of a traumatic surprise? Where were you when you got the news of the attacks on the World Center and the Pentagon? When you got the news that a loved one was diagnosed with critical illness? How do you respond when you get the news of a traumatic event, personal or global?

Initially, many experience disbelief, fear, anger, helplessness, but often a quick desire to *do* something. Context makes such a difference. In the same moment, one person engages in an heroic act of compassion while another reacts with rage. Many are moved to give financially, some to organize the work of those who help directly. Others are paralyzed by the shock for months, even years.

I recall exactly where I was the day President John F. Kennedy was shot on November 22, 1963: in my Penn State dorm room. I can still hear my Republican mother's passion overriding politics on the phone that night: "Our own president has been assassinated."

I recall exactly where I was when I got the call that my thirty-one-year-old brother David had died of a tractor accident on March 28, 1971: stranded in strange church kitchen at a regional youth production of Andrew Lloyd Webber's *Jesus Christ, Superstar*. When a friend drove me to my parents' home, my traumatized mother momentarily mistook the friend for my wife, Freddy.

When I received the news of the attacks on September 11, 2001, I was in the hallway at Pittsburgh Theological Seminary, returning from a morning break to teach a weeklong seminar on "The Soul of Tomorrow's Church." The world then became our curriculum.

Sometimes trauma disables one's memory until a safe environment is found. To recollect and tell a single traumatic story in a healing environment can tap a vein of remembering one's dismembered emotions. By speaking of them with others, the human psyche yearns to siphon up some serendipitous moment of healing and hope.

JOSEPHINE HARRIS: THE UPSIDE-DOWN MYSTERY

With severe walking disabilities, Josephine Harris began trudging her way down from about the eightieth floor of the World Trade Center, when a Ladder 6 rescue worker found her and began assisting her. Other Ladder 6 members refused to abandon their fellow rescuer to resume their rapid-paced descent. So step by laborious step the little group made its way until reaching the fourth floor. There Ms. Harris collapsed. She could go no further. She felt cold. One fireman gave her his coat. What to do? They would not leave her. Cell phones would not work in the local area. But one worker did reach his wife in New Jersey, quickly telling her to call Fire House No. 12 with their location—just as his batteries died. Then the whole tower collapsed—except for the stairwell.

Had these firemen left Josephine behind to descend faster, all would have died. She was rescued first, the workers later. It took several days to discover if Josephine survived. When Ladder 6 threw a dinner honoring Josephine, they gave her their official coat and dubbed her their Guardian Angel; she called them her Guardian Angels. She saved them and they saved her—a primodern story of interactive grace.

How dare we tell such a story when so many were *not* rescued? But how dare we *not* tell the story? How dare we tell it while innocent people with dark skins or Arab-sounding names are being profiled and arrested without cause, as I write? How dare we tell it when news of nameless ones who died from AIDS and heart attacks on September 11 was eclipsed by the attacks?

This is what I tell myself: *Finally it comes down to this for me. If I find myself alive and not dead, I have no more viable response to catastrophic surprise than to live with gratitude and compassion. To live in bitterness and resentment is the way of death.*

LEFT BEHIND?

"One will be taken and the other left." So Tim LaHaye and Jerry Jenkins twist Jesus' words in their best-selling *Left Behind* series, to scare us into believing in an apocalyptic "rapture" where true believers will be plucked from their car seats and office desks and taken to heaven while everybody else gets left behind.

As I see it, one was taken and the other left at the World Trade Center that fateful day, but not because one had more faith and the other less. Jodi is a survivor, while others are murdered victims—not because she was better or others worse. I want to show Tim LaHaye a hard copy of Jesus' words about those Galileans whose blood Pilate mingled with their sacrifices:

> "Do you think that because these Galileans suffered in this way they were worse sinners than all other Galileans? No, I tell you. . . . Or those eighteen who were killed when the tower of Siloam fell on them—do you think that they were worse offenders than all the others living in Jerusalem? No, I tell you. . . ."

TWO WAYS TO UNDERSTAND TRAUMATIC SURPRISE

I have made a distinction between shock and serendipity, two forms of surprise. Our human response to each has elements of distortion and disorientation. Each has potential for transformation or destruction. How we respond makes the difference.

Consider how studies of dysfunctional individuals and family systems give us insight into prevention of illness. But the opposite approach is also valid: to study exceptional individuals and family systems can give us insight into the positive qualities that promote health. The first focuses on pathology, the second on wholeness.

The first method, focusing on dysfunction, is illustrated in Alice Miller's work. In *The Untouched Key* and *For Your Own Good: Hidden Cruelty in Child-Rearing and the Roots of Violence,* Miller shows how Adolf Hitler's hatred of Jews stemmed in part from abuse by his own father—which the young Adolf associated with his father's Jewishness. What if Adolf could have learned to love the part of himself he hated? In *The Drama of the Gifted Child,* Miller shows how unhealed childhood traumas created potential for brilliance in the lives of Frederick Nietzsche and Nobel Prize–winner Hermann Hesse—whose book *Siddhartha* is still a classic integration of Eastern and Western spirituality.

For the second method, focusing on the exceptional, two examples come to mind. In his book *Creating Minds: An Anatomy of Creativity Seen Through the Lives of Freud, Einstein, Picasso, Stravinsky, Eliot, Graham, and Gandhi,* Howard Gardner focuses on the qualities that foster creativity. And in *The Soul's Code,* James Hillman looks at the lives of such exceptional people as Franklin Roosevelt, Eleanor Roosevelt, and Ella Fitzgerald to illustrate his acorn theory: that exceptional people have within them from childhood the seed of some destiny that survives even against great odds.

QUALITIES OF SHOCK AND SERENDIPITY

We can use these two approaches as ways of responding to traumatic or inspiring surprise. There is value in analyzing tragedy itself and human pathology, even if to learn the negative lessons of what not to do, where not to go.

The stories of Flannery O'Connor are full of terrifying upside-down moments of grace in extreme situations. As in "A Good Man Is Hard to Find" or "Revelation," the message is always clear: Don't wait for a car crash or a shotgun, or for a book to bang you in the head, before you wake up. You can choose to wake up *now!*

> As Rabbi Harold Kushner demonstrated in *When Bad Things Happen to Good People,* to choose life is to learn ways of responding creatively rather than destructively to life's pain. It is what Plato meant by the education of desire.

"On August 14, 1982, the stars fell from my sky," writes Ann Weems in *Psalms of Lament,* as she grieves her son's needless mugging and violent death. She shares her posttraumatic shock prayer with all:

> In the godforsaken, obscene quicksand of life,
> there is a deafening alleluia
> rising from the souls
> of those who weep,
> and of those who weep with those who weep.
> If you watch, you will see
> the hand of God
> putting the stars back in their skies
> one by one.

Reflection Exercise 17. Create Your Own Psalm of Lament

Psalms in the Bible invite us to offer our raw, uncensored emotions to the Holy One. (An example: "My God, my God, why have you forsaken me?" [Psalm 22].) Ponder a situation of stress, anger, or sadness. Now write (or draw, paint, carve, or sculpt) your own honest-to-God psalmlike yearnings and groanings. An idea: if your work is on a flat surface, overlay it with the word *Love,* using pastels, light tissue paper, or another medium. An option: use the same exercise to create a psalm focused on joy, ecstasy, or beauty.

11

YOU ARE DUST. YOU ARE STARS!

Two Keys

The presence of the star does not excuse us from the difficult territory through which it is guiding us.
—DAVID WHYTE, CROSSING THE UNKNOWN SEA

Through her tears, Sylvia told me of breathing the dust and human ashes that lined the Manhattan streets and laced her Brooklyn windowsills on September 11. She told of choking her way to a synagogue that week, after not attending for years, and how the mourner's *Kaddish* prayer broke her heart open.

Overnight, Rowan Williams (now the archbishop of Canterbury) scrapped his prepared lecture for September 12, 2001, at the Cathedral of St. John the Divine. Instead, he shared heart-wrenching reflections, later gathered in a small book, *Writing in the Dust.*

A rabbi recites: "I carry two keys. The key in one pocket says, 'You are but dust and ashes.' In the other it says, 'For you the universe was created!'" To grovel in self-pity or gloat in self-importance is to endanger life's vital balance.

All this got me thinking a lot about the mystery of dust. California potter Sasha Makovkin explains how the dust of ancient pulverized rocks is the source of clay for his beautiful ceramic chalices. He queries how the nomadic Hebrews' clothing would have made them aware of their dustiness.

One night I received a call that my older cousin had died suddenly. At his grave I proclaimed, "Dust to dust, ashes to ashes"—and felt the gritty words in my throat. Yet over coffee after the funeral, an amazing gift of life was born. My cousin's grieving son and I felt a connection. (I had last seen him at age twelve, at my wedding.) Now we regularly share our lives and dreams. A self-described spiritual orphan, he is the younger brother I never had, coming forth astonishingly, phoenixlike, out of the ashes.

THE BUDDHA MYTH—AND OUR OWN

"Life is difficult." So begins M. Scott Peck's classic *The Road Less Traveled*. Dr. Benjamin Spock's *Baby and Child Care* opens with: "You know more than you think you do." These first lines from two twentieth-century best-sellers capture the essential human paradox. Peck's line paraphrases the first of the Buddha's four noble truths: "Life is suffering." Spock's line expresses the bold ideal of human possibility.

Without explicitly religious language and with unvarnished simplicity, these two lines embody the truth that life is out of sync, yet also full of possibility and hope. Pascal spoke of knowing one's baseness and one's greatness. Life seems awful, other times awesome, and sometimes a serendipitous infusion of both.

The Buddha's myth shows how we cannot find fulfillment apart from suffering *(dukkha)*. Growing up in a privileged household, the youthful Gautama was never to see suffering. He married well and was prosperous. But like the Garden of Eden, an ideal ethos is a setup for the opposite. In his twenties, he became restless. He left home to follow the worldly path of pleasures and success.

Later he tried self-denying ascetic practices, yet still found no peace. At one point, he recalled a forgotten childhood epiphany. He saw himself filled with wonder sitting under an ancient Bodhi tree. What led to such bliss? He then recalled it had been a day of celebration when farmers plowed the first earth of the season. He was deeply moved to see worms cut and plowed underground. This sense of compassion preceded the sense of wonder and oneness with all creation as he sat under the Bodhi tree.

The Buddha's story teaches us about genuine spiritual experience: any lasting peace is linked to "compassion" (in Latin, "suffering with"). In Hebrew the word for compassion is *racham,* related to the word for womb. In Greek the word for compassion is *splagchna,* bowels. Peace that is *real* is born out of gut-wrenching experiences.

The Buddha myth is ours. We leave home to find home again. To get to the stage of knowing more than you think you do, you have to enter the difficulty more deeply. Some disorientation must happen on the way to a reorientation. You break your back and brain and heart; that's when a forgotten line drops into your life to give you direction.

I am convinced every person has a treasury of such gems of experience, where one line has dropped from the ceiling. Yet many fail to see it drop, or feel the wonder of it, or find a safe place to speak of it. It just lies there, long buried. Simply to recall one such buried gem of spiritual awareness can give us guidance.

In *The Sacred Journey,* Frederick Buechner writes, "These are moments of crazy, holy grace—crazy because they come from somewhere farther than Oz, and holy because they heal and hallow our broken lives."

MOST DIFFICULT READING, MOST AUTHENTIC

A member of my family was assigned to a difficult site in the health care world. While visiting her at the Frank Lloyd Wright home Falling Water in western Pennsylvania, we opened a book to find Wright's prescription for a contemporary home: "First, pick a good site. Pick that one at the most difficult site—pick a site no one wants—but pick one that has features making for character: trees, individuality, a fault of some kind in the realtor mind."

We looked at each other—and knew the secret of her difficult worksite. Wright had stated a simple, profound paradox: that the very fault in your life can itself become a place of beauty. Spiritual traditions want to move us from knowing "about" this reality to knowing the Reality itself as myths and rituals come alive in such drops of experience (see Chapter Fifteen).

Bruce Metzger, one of the world's leading New Testament textual critics, studied many centuries-old Greek and Syriac papyri. His conclusion: the most difficult reading of a text is usually most authentic. The reason: scribes down through centuries tended to edit a difficult text as they copied it to remove its ambiguities, smooth out the inconsistencies.

I ponder how the most difficult reading of one's life is often the most authentic place of growth. We tend to suppress traumatic experiences because of the pain. Today as I read Alice Miller's *The Drama of the Gifted Child,* I see my early childhood traumas and illness exposed and redeemed, revalued.

As an adult, I contemplate the posttraumatic shock from two (out of four) congregations where I entered as a starry-eyed Lone Ranger and left broken-hearted. Images still haunt my dreams. Yet the wounds created the vocational treasure that nurtures my spiritual development ministry and writing.

> "Life is difficult." This is the human condition. "You know more than you think." This is the human potential. You are star dust.

This is the meaning of Godspel, "good news": the difficulties of life can become a doorway to a deeper kind of knowing, a movement beyond rationality to spirituality. Pascal said, "The heart has reasons that reason knows nothing about."

Reflection Exercise 18. What Is Sabbath for You?

In your journal, reflect on Rainer Maria Rilke's words: "I am the rest / between two notes / which are somehow / always in discord." Journal with these questions:

What are the two notes in discord for you? (Examples: doubting and believing, health and illness, war and peace, task and relationship, work and home, caring for children and caring for aging parents)

What is the rest? Or what form does sabbath take for you?

Who is the rest? a soul friend? the Spirit? Can *you* become the rest for someone else?

Are you drawn to some rhythm of weekly rest, reading, renewal, and reflection?

Note: In Jewish tradition, *Shabbat* means rest, ceasing, especially on the seventh day of the week. We can also cultivate mini-sabbaths.

12

INSIGHT IS NOT TRANSFERABLE

Insight is not transferable.
—H. CLAYTON MOYER

It would be nice to transfer wisdom the way we can pass
food around the table.
—SOCRATES, IN THE SYMPOSIUM

Once, in my twenties, I was listening to a mentor give an after-dinner talk on communication. As an aside he said, "And as we all know, insight is not transferable." As we *all* know? I queried myself. The line never let go of me.

HOW TO FAST FROM INSIGHT: ASKING QUESTIONS

I recall a teenager in a class I taught in the sixties, sitting week by week with her head angled just so that her long hair entirely hid her face from my view—daring me to get one word or even a glance from her.

Why did it never occur to me to change my seat? Ask what movies the kids had seen? Take a minute of silence for them to think of an issue they wanted to explore? Pose a question to discuss with each other in dyads or triads? "Teachers teach as they were taught, and not as they were taught to teach" goes an old saw. Those who taught me mainly lectured, and I will say they *never* made use of silence in the classroom.

I have struggled in teaching and parenting and conversations to get others involved. Then I began to recognize for myself how I need to feel ownership in someone else's idea from the bottom up if the idea is to become my own.

"As we all know, insight is not transferable." Somewhere along life's way, it occurred to me that when I feel an insight coming on I can hold it back and fast from it a bit, to see if I can convert my insight into a *question*.

This creates three spiritual movements. First, to convert an insight into a question creates a pause in my psyche while this miniconversion takes place. Second, I momentarily lose control. By my talking, I keep another passive; I can give advice. Asking creates a pause, makes me vulnerable: Where is this going to go? Third, the other person also has to pause and ponder the question, slowing down the rapid-fire train of thought.

Turning an insight into a question works wonders in parenting, human relations, management, teaching, and life. You cannot teach the art of contemplation, yet an ordinary query can induce what the philosopher Lessing called "the creative pause." Such a pregnant moment allows for a mini-*kenosis,* a bit of empty space, like a rest in a musical score—where whatever we mean by insight or wonder or grace can creep in. Wonder working is what mystery is all about.

> In her masterpiece *Their Eyes Were Watching God,* Zora Neale Hurston writes: "There are years that ask questions and years that answer."

A young man insisted on his desire for a doctoral program, yet seemed hesitant. I was tempted to point out that he was afraid of failure. Instead, I asked, What is your deepest fear? He began with fears about money, time, and maybe failing. He paused. He then he said the whole grad school idea was really based on a fear of not measuring up to his older brother. He needed to pursue *his* vision, what he wants. Had I told my insight, he might have missed his own.

Learning to convert little ideas in conversations into questions can train us to welcome life's big questions—to live into the answer some future day. In *Big Questions, Worthy Dreams,* Sharon Daloz Parks asserts that many young adults are being cheated:

> *They are not being asked big-enough questions.* They are not being
> invited to entertain the greatest questions of their own lives
> and of their times. . . . What do I really want to become? When
> do I feel most alive? Where can I be creative? What are my
> fears? What am I vulnerable to? . . . Why is there a growing gap
> between the haves and the have-nots? Why is the prison popu-
> lation growing in the United States? Why are antidepressants
> being prescribed for increasing numbers of children? What are
> the reasons for climate change?

During my older daughter's first college interview, she quietly tried to put her best foot forward. Then one big question turned the interview on its head: "When have you experienced failure?" She came up with some answer, she later told us. But our family learned that one of life's qualifications is the ability to use failure creatively.

Questions open up insights from within and afar. Is this not what spiritual leadership is all about: coaching others to open to unknown wisdom?

HOW TO FAST FROM INSIGHT: TELLING STORIES

Every time I "die" to one of my own insights and watch it rise creatively in another, I witness a miniresurrection. Like questions, a good story creates a momentary suspension of preconceived ideas. Consider this story about Socrates, adapted from the *Symposium:*

> A friend of Socrates wins the prize for the annual plays in Athens. He throws a great party and invites Socrates to come along. Socrates pays little attention to his appearance so he usually looks grungy, but he gets himself cleaned up that day. People ask, "Is Socrates going courting?" he is so dressed up! Along the way, as sometimes happens with Socrates, he has what philosophers call a "trance" and religious folks call a "mystical experience." His friends leave him there, knowing he will soon come along. Sure enough, after a bit Socrates shows up at the party. People are already lying around the table eating but are not drunk yet. The host says, "Oh Socrates, come up here and lie down next to me, but keep your head a bit higher than mine so the wisdom that you just got out there will flow down into my head, and I will be wise like you." Socrates answers this playful remark seriously yet simply: "Oh, if only it were that easy to transfer wisdom from one head to another. It would be nice to transfer wisdom the way we pass food around the table."

Research shows that technical information stimulates the *left* sphere of the brain (the place of linguistic, logical, and linear thinking). And the *right* sphere (the place of rhythmic, artistic, creative thinking) is stimulated by music, art, and dance. But when *stories* are fed to the brain, something amazing happens: both spheres are stimulated.

The multiple-intelligences approach of Howard Gardner offers a lens to awaken the soul's true self in all arenas of life. Stories use all nine learning modes (the italicized words shown here) for mending the interrupted narratives of our lives (see Chapter Seven). Stories are vehicles for transmitting life. They contain a "storyline" employing *language,* using linear thinking and *logic.* Stories create *space* through imagination, and they often contain *music* (or they are made into musicals, operas, or ballads). Stories are *kinesthetic,* embodied in gestures, drama, and dance. Stories create *intrapersonal* movements in the heart and *interpersonal* relationships among hearers. Stories contain *naturalist* images: the mystery of devastation and renewal, violence and beauty. Finally, *existentialist* intelligence: stories tell us how we can find meaning in all the rhythms of life.

Questions and stories form the yin and the yang of learning to yearn for one's deepest desire—as in the methods of Krishna, the Buddha, Lao Tzu, Socrates, Hillel, or Jesus. A good question or a good story is more life-giving than any ready-made answer.

**"Things seen are made
from things unseen."**

When I hold back an insight,
      another speaks the word;
When I ache to give an answer but there is
      none, hope is conceived;
When I yearn to express an idea and there are
      no words, a story is born;
When I lead by stepping back,
      others' gifts come forth.

SPIRITUAL LAB EXPERIMENTS

I quip how I used to have three theories of parenting, but after rearing three children I have no more theories left. Parenting is the art of transferring insight indirectly. "Tell all the truth, but tell it slant," wrote Emily Dickinson. The bankruptcy of lots of educational and human relations theories comes from assuming that insight *is* transferable. What if we turned the strategy upside down, so life was more laboratory than lecture?

Prayer is to spirituality what the laboratory is to science: the place for testing traditional hypotheses and experimenting with new ones. Your fingers get burned, beakers explode, and

> Turn this saying on its head: "Don't just stand there, do something" becomes "Don't just do something, stand there." We often equate believing with doing, when in fact nonaction might become the creed—and the deed.

your hands get cut. Observing my first autopsy as a chaplain, I thought I would throw up.

But you never forget the experience. You go back to life and it explodes with an "Aha!"—accompanied by blood, sweat, and tears. In *Women Who Run with the Wolves,* Clarissa Pinkola Estés writes: "I hope you will go out and let stories happen to you, and that you will work with them, water them with your blood and tears and your laughter till they bloom, till you yourself burst into bloom. Then you will see what medicines they make, and where and when to apply them. That is the work. The only work."

A SAFE ENVIRONMENT FOR HEALING STORIES

Sitting in a restaurant in Buffalo with a newly discovered relative of my mother's family, we spoke of our common ancestor, Henry Bull, who was governor of Rhode Island under the British Crown in the 1690s. But for the first time I learned our ancestor was a Quaker who had befriended the women's leader Ann Hutchinson, aiding her flight from Massachusetts where she was attacked as a witch. I understood our family's intense interest in women's rights.

What keeps us from hungering for these healing stories? Is it fear of betrayal? Is it fear of skeletons in our family closet? Is it that we are exiled from our ancestors?

Orphaned from our own broken blessed family stories, we are cut off from part of our original blessing. Salvation includes coming home to your own genetic and family roots. Sometimes a person may need a story more than food to stay alive.

"There are so many stories, / more beautiful than answers," wrote Mary Oliver in *House of Light*. Given a safe environment such as a home or retreat setting, I am amazed at how folks who do not know each other—and some who think they do—find themselves awestruck by each other's stories. A trusting spiritual community is formed from the web of people's half-forgotten scripts.

After a family visited in our home one evening, when we stepped outside the Big Dipper seemed so bright; I mentioned how I liked to find the North Star, Polaris, by sighting upward from the two stars on the end of the dipper. Another told how slaves escaping on the Underground Railroad would teach their children to sing, "Follow the Drinking Gourd" so they could always find their way north. Sadly, neither the parents nor their young African American son had ever heard this part of their own story.

The job of spiritual leaders is to organize safe environments to learn through the chemistry of people's own broken beakers and aha experiments. Invite them to their long-buried treasures. Healing stories empower people to risk new explorations.

Storied Truth
To cradle a new insight or give
birth to anything ever lasting:
wrap your truth in stories.

The root meaning of *e-ducare* in Latin means to lead out. Jesus embodied *educare*—this art of evoking insight—in his quadruplet teaching methods: stories, questions, pithy koan-like proverbs, and the power of example.

Seeker: What can I do to get eternal life?
Teacher (answering question with question): How do *you* read the Law?

Seeker: Love God and your neighbor.

Teacher: Do this and you will live forever right now!

Seeker: OK, but who is my neighbor?

Teacher: A tourist goes down from Jerusalem to Jericho and gets mugged by robbers. A minister, a priest, an imam, and a rabbi each drive right on by. But a suspected terrorist comes along and rescues the traveler. So what do you think?

Which was neighbor to the one that got mugged?

Seeker: Uh, the guy who showed compassion, of course.

Teacher: Go and do likewise.

We get wounded like the tourist in this story, who did a foolish thing—setting out *alone* on a road known to be dangerous. So each of us has daredevilishly taken some lonely road. But the attackers were *not* of the traveler's doing; he was also wounded by the circumstances—the wrong place, at the wrong time. We are often wounded by some combination of foolish things we do and external circumstances beyond our control.

But we are saved by surprise: compassion does not always come from the expected sources—institutional religion, spiritual leaders. Some of our woundings actually come from rejections when religious institutions "pass us by on the other side."

It is strangely inspiring to know that gifted spiritual mentors—Pascal, Kierkegaard, Sojourner Truth, Simone Weil, Dorothy Day—were bypassed and had a lover's quarrel with their own religion. Divine compassion often comes through the hands of a "smarting Samaritan" (updated as a suspected terrorist in my retelling of Jesus' parable). Jesus turned a religious question about heaven into a spiritual political encounter.

Leaders like Jesus embodied the example by hanging out with people who were not socially safe. Gandhi reportedly said, "My life is my message." It is true we learn from our teachers. But our teachers are often mysteriously hidden in the lives of the people we are called to serve.

WHY ANOTHER BOOK—OR LECTURE?

If we cannot pass wisdom around the table the way we do food, then why do I write this book, or teach? Even though insight is not directly transferable, the desire for it is. It can be prompted by a deep love of the subject, the lure of the teller's example, or a traumatic surprise in one's life.

Since his tragic spinal cord injury, Christopher Reeve has devoured research on the nervous system, something that never interested him before. Now some of us take up the cause of Reeve's compassionate insights because of his well-known example. But no one planned Reeve's traumatic surprise of being thrown from a horse one beautiful Virginia morning. His life is full of pain and wonder and mystery.

G. K. Chesterton, an English journalist who in his early life was an agnostic, wrote: "At the back of our brains, so to speak, there is a forgotten blaze or burst of astonishment at our existence. The object of the spiritual life is to dig for this submerged sunrise of wonder." You cannot transfer wisdom like food, but you can practice being awake to the surprise of a submerged sunrise.

Reflection Exercise 19. Practicing Questions, Telling Stories

Seize occasions to experiment in the coming week. Try making an observation or asking a question instead of giving an insight: "I noticed a phrase you used (repeating what the person said); I wonder, what's that about?" Or if a story comes to mind more than once while conversing, share it. Gently ask if there might be any connection for the other person. Allow pauses to draw you deeper into trusting love in the Ground of your being.

Reflection Exercise 20. Turn an Idea on Its Head!

If you have trouble understanding someone's question or idea (or one of your own), ask: What happens when you turn it on its head? word it in an opposite way? (An example: people are always asking an unemployed or depressed person, "Why don't you get out of the house and get a job?" A possible alternative might be: "Can you think of a way to get out of your house and stay at home at the same time?") Wait for the reply. Then come back to the original idea. Ask the person you are with (or yourself): "Did you sense any shift? any surprise insight as you came back to the original idea?" Meditate. Practice this, using sample questions in your journal. Converse about it with someone.

MYSTERY

Inklings of Transformation

The world breaks every one and afterward
many are strong at the broken places.
—ERNEST HEMINGWAY, A FAREWELL TO ARMS

Struggle changes us; it grows us up.
—JOAN D. CHITTISTER, SCARRED BY STRUGGLE, TRANSFORMED BY HOPE

Beauty throws a curve ball.
—KEITH WILSON, MUSICIAN

13

THE MURDER OF MYSTERY

Life is not a problem to be solved but a mystery to be
explored.
—GABRIEL MARCEL

The central mystery is still novel: that barriers can become
bridges to wholeness and holiness. So why do we kill off
the mystery instead of exploring it?

DEEPENING MYSTERY VERSUS HAVING ANSWERS

A church's outdoor sign boasted, "Christ is the Answer!" Then
someone sprayed graffiti: "But what's the question?" One of the
dangers of fundamentalist forms of religion—or politics or science or any realm of life—is the compulsion to give quick
answers with no shades of gray.

One can find a simplistic answer for any complex problem, neatly packaged, easily believable—and mostly wrong. With
a little more doubting, there would be a lot less killing. Too
much certitude or analysis closes things down. Mystery opens
things up.

"As soon as mystery is scheduled for solution, it is no longer a mystery; it is a problem," Wendell Berry wrote in *Life Is a Miracle*. A twentysomething friend meditated on Berry's words and shared his journal entry with me: "To assert that we can explain, reduce, attain, possess, manipulate, what is truly sacred, divine and beyond knowing is to blaspheme. The murder of mystery is to close the door on possibility beyond our minute human scope."

Our military technological political machines murder the mystery. Barbara Kingsolver reflects in *Small Wonder* how fewer monarch butterflies are now making their annual trek to Mexico because of chemical effects on pollen. Huge agribusinesses market chemically altered seed to poor countries—seed that is timed to expire—to replace ancient seed that would normally sprout even after centuries. Wordsworth speaks about this murder of mystery in a superrational culture:

> Sweet is the lore which Nature brings;
> Our meddling intellect
> Mis-shapes the beauteous forms of things:
> We murder to dissect.

THE COSMIC MYSTERY: PERSONAL AND POLITICAL

Mystery is the ideal metaphor for our sleuthing project because it has exactly the secular and spiritual connotations I want to mine and combine: mystery as in the lure of Sherlock Holmes or Agatha Christie stories sleuthing for clues of insight, and mystery as in a great Mystery hidden at the heart of the universe, the *mysterium tremendum*.

Contemporary mysteries like Stephen King's *The Shining* add a primodern dimension: several mysteries happen simultaneously, coupling primal experience—the grandmother's ancestral aura, which she called "the shining"—with modern technological filming techniques.

In the world of science, it is accepted that any genuine discovery creates a new edge of mystery. In the world of religion any genuine way leads to the mystery of transforming Love at the heart of existence.

Sadly, fundamentalists preach rigid answers that divide people, and they ignore the New Testament's political–social dimensions of "the mystery of Christ," who "has made both groups into one and has broken down the dividing wall, that is the hostility between us." The world saw a glimpse of this mystery incarnated in October 1989 as the Berlin Wall was dismantled piece by piece to singing and dancing. Likewise in South Africa, humanity witnessed how *apartheid*—hate that drove people apart—was dissembled without a major bloody war.

Mysteriously, novel solutions to injustice are still rising out of religious and political rubble. "This One is our peace"— *incognito,* without a name, or by any name—wherever such renewing mystery happens.

UNDERGROUND GRACE

"The world breaks every one and afterward many are strong at the broken places." This is the gospel according to Hemingway. Finding a secular spirituality, one that does not need to posit a God out there in order to find faith, has everything to do with the mystery of paying attention to the blessed broken stuff in your own life and in the world.

The popular Jewish author Jonathan Kozol captures glimpses of transforming mystery in *Ordinary Resurrections,* stories about inklings of light in the lives of disenfranchised children of Harlem. They become his, and our, tutors and guides.

Some glorious mystery resides on the edges, hovers over the brokenness, hangs out at the bottoms of things. This is why worldly mystics, such as Francis of Assisi or Gandhi, Dorothy Day or Mother Teresa, have always stayed close to the marginalized, *les miserables*, the *anawim* in Hebrew, the least of these, where Messiah is to be found.

This mysterious underground grace can take raw abuse and half-repressed shame and transform it into life-giving resiliency. Often it is *sub*liminal, just beneath the threshold (*limen* in Latin) of awareness. Such half-submerged inklings of grace may contain hidden monsters as well as stars of light. "These resurrected gems are bridgeheads into alien territory," wrote R. D. Laing in *The Politics of Experience*. They call us back to our true home while on the journey. Falling and rising at the margins of life, we come to the center.

A Beautiful Mind portrays the real-life mystery of Princeton mathematician John Forbes Nash Jr., whose brilliant career is persistently invaded by acute schizophrenia. The off-the-wall professor teaches us to pay attention to marginal people. Treat mental illness with respect, Nash would remind us, because the voices he hears come from the same mysterious place as the insights for his Nobel Prize–winning gaming theory. Nash's astounding craziness is a reminder to notice my attitude with persons I might quickly write off.

MYSTERY: A WALL BECOMES A BRIDGE

E. L. Doctorow was sitting in his study in New Rochelle, New York, in 1972, unable to write. He could only stare at the wall. So he started writing about the wall. . . . Then he wrote about the house the wall was attached to: a three-story brown shingle with dormers, . . . built in 1906, the start of an optimistic new century. President Teddy Roosevelt had just sent the U.S. fleet around the world. Women carried white parasols; men wore white skimmers. It was a cozy self-satisfied America, where Negroes, Indians, and immigrants were invisible. In Doctorow's imagination the wall exploded into a whole new multicultural world that we know as a book, a movie, and a musical named *Ragtime*.

Sometimes you break down the wall to create peace. Other times the wall becomes a link to creative imagination. In *Gravity and Grace,* the French activist and philosopher Simone Weil speaks of the Greek concept of *metaxu,* or bridge: how the barrier may become the passageway. She uses the example of how walls in a prisoner-of-war camp are quickly transformed into bridges of communication as prisoners tap out codes to each other.

But we often destroy the barriers and murder the mystery. We knock down whatever gets in the way of what we think we want—nations, things, nature, people—as if they were devils when really they might be angels of annunciation.

Reflection Exercise 21. Group Experiment with Focusing

Try this experiment, especially with a group of young people. Ask for a volunteer to sit in the center of the circle, blindfolded. Request the rest to focus their energies on the blindfolded one, whom you ask to report any change. In a few minutes, give an inaudible signal to release the focus. Wait a minute for the blindfolded person (who usually feels the shift) to report. Ask: If we can experience normal human energies across a room, why not in Germany? or Ghana? Were they thinking of love as they focused their energies? What are the connections with prayer or meditation?

For further reading, see Larry Dossey, *Recovering the Soul: A Scientific and Spiritual Search* (New York: Bantam Books, 1989).

14

"YOU SHOULD SEE MT. ST. HELENS NOW!"

Nothing is worse than a wasted crisis.
—ANONYMOUS MYSTIC

While I was leading a seminar at Chautauqua, New York, participants were discussing how negative events, over time, can create positive imprints. A young adult from Seattle leaned forward and said, "You should see Mt. St. Helens now!"

One of the most devastating volcanoes to erupt in the United States in recent times rained fire and ash in 1980. In the moment of hearing "You should see Mt. St. Helens now!" we knew the reality that life has a propensity toward transformation and renewal.

SLEUTHING FOR ARTIFACTS OF GRACE

The theme of mystery moves to the deepest level of worldly holiness. Over time, even abrasive bits of life can transform nature and nations and human existence. We are sleuthing for clues to faith, hope, and love buried in the mysterious grit of life.

Sleuth comes from an old Scandinavian word meaning "track," a creature's imprint on the trail, or trek. As such, life experiences often leave their imprints, which at the time can feel like something very sharp and stressful bearing in from beyond. But in a time when one needs reorientation, the harsh imprints can serve as artifacts of grace to detect some sort of movement in our lives.

Given the tincture of time and a safe environment where we can befriend them, these imprints offer us a sense of orientation: Why was I going that direction? What was happening outside my life? inside my life? What direction do I need to move in now?

INKLINGS OF TRANSFORMATION

J.R.R. Tolkien, C. S. Lewis, Dorothy Sayers, and other writers dubbed themselves "Inklings." First, they valued their actual written inklings from pen and ink—doodled on fragments of placemats or brown paper bags. Sometimes all a writer gets from a whole day's work is one creative scribbling. Second, these Oxford writers knew that in this world of "middle earth" we are fortunate just to get inklings of transformation—bits and pieces of beauty or wholeness popping through our wildest experiences of success and struggle.

Just an inkling could spawn a whole fantasy series, as with Tolkien's *The Fellowship of the Ring* or Lewis's *The Chronicles of Narnia,* or complex mystery novels such as Dorothy Sayers's *Lord Peter Wimsey* series.

FREDERICK DOUGLASS AND KEYS TO TRANSFORMATION

Struggle is the midwife of transformation. One inkling of grace is enough to reorient a life and recreate hope.

Frederick Douglass, a child slave who would become a brilliant educator, overheard his master warn that it was a dangerous thing to let slaves learn to read and write. With that single inkling, the youthful Douglass determined to master the alphabet. Through keen observation he had already learned four letters, and he boasted that he could draw them better than white boys. They taunted him, "Betcha don't know the next letter!" He would endure their shaming until he had tricked yet another letter out of his youthful oppressors, finally winning the treasure that would be his doorway to freedom.

Here is the deep mystery at the heart of existence: How can destructive events, emotions, and experiences be used creatively? Grace cannot be programmed, but we can detect from Douglass's story certain clues that create the openness to these inklings of transformed reality:

- *Show up.* Woody Allen said 80 percent of life is showing up. Be present to life's joy or pain—even enemies, like Douglass with his master.
- *Pay attention.* Here is the essence of the Hebrew *Shema* that Jesus endorsed: Listen to Love, to love. Eastern traditions call it mindfulness. Be awake to each moment, to things that disturb as well as delight you. What if Douglass had not paid attention to the master's offhand warning?
- *Be open to surprise—serendipity or shock.* Any experience may contain the potential for transformation, as illustrated by Douglass's pivotal incident.
- *Follow through.* Every spiritual tradition has a word meaning "follower" or "disciple," implying a pilgrimage and obstacles. Douglass not only paid attention but also followed through on his dream, even at the risk of being shamed.
- *Ask questions, tell stories.* A good question can plant a seed in the soul and birth a story. Douglass converted his master's comment into a dangerous question: What if I *do* learn to read? That became the acorn for his life of education and action.

- *Cultivate humor. Humor,* like *humus,* is born out of the low places. People laugh and cry reading about "the Irish misery" in Frank McCourt's *Angela's Ashes.* Comedians develop humor as their ally because often as kids they were lonely or shy. To acquire the treasure of the alphabet, Douglass created a game; he chose to be a holy fool, temporarily allowing himself to be the butt of white kids' jokes.
- *Befriend emptiness.* Questions, stories, and humor all have a way of creating a minitrance, a momentary pause, a temporary suspension of disbelief. At other times it is a prolonged night of the soul, sometimes self-chosen, sometimes imposed by circumstances. Like Douglass's yearning for a new thing to be born, the gestation period creates a fantasy riddled with fear: Where will this take me?

> As with Frederick Douglass, a mysterious "underground grace" can bring to surface a dangerous question or comment, one that contains the acorn to transform your life. You can recognize it because it seems wonderful and scary at the same time.

"Nothing is worse than a wasted crisis," wrote an anonymous mystic. Spirituality is the art of mining raw underground gems of frozen apathy or red-hot anger so they can be transformed to refract the light.

Reflection Exercise 22. Listening to a Radio Station as a Prayer

Here is a way to walk in the moccasins of a loved one or friend you want to understand better: listen to that person's favorite radio station. (Or read a book or see a movie the person would like—by yourself, or together.) Maybe you will converse about it, maybe not. But if it helps you understand your friend, then it is prayer. (In tradition, it would be called an *intercessory* prayer, that is, your soul's concern offered on behalf of another.)

Reflection Exercise 23. Sounds of Technology, of Nature, of Silence

Find a really noisy place outside, like a bench near a shopping mall parking lot or an expressway. Sit . . . observe colors, light, movements . . . close your eyes and slow down your breathing. Notice the sounds of technology (cars, planes, radios). . . . Then see if you can hear even faint sounds of nature (birds, insects, wind) . . . . Finally, listen beyond the noises to the sound of silence. If you can't, just invite the distractions in as prayers. Conclude by opening your eyes and reflecting on this experience. An option: turn up music loudly to practice the same exercise at your own home (inside or outside—but give some thought to your neighbors!).

15

THE MATRIX

Through Anger to Forgiveness to Freedom

Nothing in life is wasted. Without garbage we could not
have flowers.
—THICH NHAT HANH

Apathy is frozen rage.
—MARY, CHICAGO, 1969

I will never forget Mary's "teaching" in the wake of riots and
assassinations in the late 1960s. Recruited from the streets of
westside Chicago to educate us minister-types for urban ministry, Mary would say, "Apathy is frozen rage." Like a liturgical
refrain, during this monthlong program whenever anyone
recounted a surprise incident of violence, we would hear it
again: "Like I say, apathy's just frozen rage."

About a month later, I took a course on "The Psychology
of Education" at the Univer-
sity of Chicago from Allison
Davis, author of a classic
series on descendants of
slaves, *The Eighth Generation*.
(I recall my delight two

"After my divorce," Pat said, "I
was angry with God; then I felt
guilty for being angry, so I
stayed away from church."

decades later when he was featured on an African American heritage stamp.) The class could be summed up in Davis's repeated phrase: "Depression is anger turned inward." It sounded only a tad more scholarly and Freudian than Mary's refrain; I was sure the two had colluded.

MOVING THROUGH ANGER TO FORGIVENESS: HEALING RITUALS

Healing is more than mere personal good feeling; it involves relationships. Here is a great mystery of the spiritual life: How can destructive experiences metamorphose into life-giving gifts in community? In *Praying Your Goodbyes,* Joyce Rupp outlines four stages, as I summarize them.

Recognition of the hurt and fear beneath the rage or resentment is the beginning step. Only by being aware and naming the demons can they be offered to become what the Greeks called the *daemon,* a source of positive energy. *Reflection* makes use of meditating, praying, and journaling. *Ritualization* involves repetitive practices—spiritual and physical, verbal and visual, as I explore later. All of these help move to the fourth stage, the goal: *reorientation.* I see all four wrapped up in the concept of relinquishment.

People love to give advice:"You should just let go!" I want to scream, "But *how?*" Rituals can provide the *how* for relinquishing, so that our lives can be reoriented, re-Eastered. As Robert Fulghum demonstrates in his best-seller *From Beginning to End: The Rituals of Our Lives,* creative ritual embodies life-giving potential.

There are occasions, through the incidence of time or surprise timings, when one-to-one reconciliation happens. (Twelve Step programs like Alcoholics Anonymous encourage such reconciliations.) That is golden. Once a man's eye fell on a name in an out-of-town paper, and he penned a note to a person he had been estranged from for more than a decade. It prompted a mutual forgiveness. Chance encounters at restaurants, concerts, or sports events can open the aperture for candid reconcilitations.

Family rituals can heal, or hurt. Debbie had a stormy relationship with her stepmother, Joan. Early in Debbie's marriage to Keith, at Christmas dinner with her father and Joan in Arizona, the phone rang: it was Joan's adopted daughter calling from Florida. When Joan came back to the table, she said with deep emotion, "You'll never know till it happens to you how much it means to get a call from your daughter on a holiday."

Years later, after Debbie's father's funeral, Joan completely broke off her relationship with Debbie, Keith, and their young children. Months passed. Keith kept pondering what he later called the "divine line" at the dinner table. Then on the next holiday they called Joan and wished her well. It broke the ice. Joan resumed her rituals of remembering her step-grandchildren at birthdays and holidays, until her death years later.

But other times there may be no closure. A person dies or disappears. This is when rituals can help. I may write an unsent letter, burn a letter, converse with a person not present using an empty chair, name the gifts that came out of a negative relationship, find and meditate on an object of nature that represents my feelings. Or I write my way through the pain, using a dialogue in my journal. Or act it out. Or do physical exercise, like tai chi or yoga. Or talk it out with a confidant.

After leaving a toxic work situation, I felt angry with a few people who seemed unable to express their discontent constructively. Feeling incapable of forgiveness, I pondered words of Jesus from the cross: "Abba, forgive them; for they do not know what they are doing." (People hurt you but do not know they hurt themselves too.) When I feel unable to forgive, I open my arms in a cruciform position, imagine Jesus' words cycling around in me, breathe deeply several times, and with a final exhalation drop my hands.

TRANSFORMATION OF ANGER INTO A SOCIAL CAUSE: A MORE EXCELLENT WAY

Transforming negative experiences for a social value happens through *sublimation*—which differs radically from *suppression*. Suppression means stuffing your feelings, unawares. Then you explode—or wither. But creative sublimation means paying attention to the original pain, emotionally, physically, spiritually (as I've just suggested in naming some possible ritualistic acts). Then you follow an intentional course of action to channel negative energies into a positive cause.

MADD (Mothers Against Drunk Driving) exists because the families of victims of car crashes turn their anger toward positive change in public awareness and safety. Mahatma Gandhi and Martin Luther King Jr. understood well this spiritual art of sublimation; their anger at injustice was healed only through their lifelong process of social transformation. A friend tells me this is the basic principle of community organization.

Ultimately this process of creative sublimation is not something we *do* at all, but a transformation worked in us. By practicing repeated habits of noticing our emotions and offering them in prayer and meditation, we can claim the reality of St. Augustine's wisdom: "Hope has two beautiful daughters, Anger and Courage. Anger that things are the way they are. Courage to make them what they ought to be."

In the film *The Matrix,* Thomas is transformed when he begins to doubt the dehumanizing matrix surrounding his work. His anger at the system then causes him to listen to the (phone) call to freedom.

LIFE IS FORE-GIVING AND FORGIVING

I arrived early one Sunday at a church I was serving, to fill the baptismal font with water. An usher bounded toward me to "confess" how he had declined to sell his house to an African

American family. Protestant pastors are not taught to handle confessionals, especially on the spot. I recall feeling as helpless as he felt, yet touched by his vulnerability. Standing at the baptismal font dumbfounded, I think I blurted out something like God would forgive him, but he had better be careful not to miss the next chance to act on the courage of his convictions. I have since heard these words for myself.

Reflecting on this, it has occurred to me that whatever I mean by faith is basically a commitment *then* to give away the faith *now*. It is a commitment to fore-giving, as when, in a moment, I offer to buy someone's lunch without even a hint of thinking I will get it back. So much of my anger comes from calculating "what's in this for me"—which murders the mystery of fore-giving and forgiving.

An Orthodox priest served as a chaplain for the local county prison. He told me of an inmate who had burglarized a church, who asked Father Jon if he would contact the church to ask for forgiveness. The church's pastor answered that his official board would have to vote on the matter. After several weeks, Father Jon called and the pastor reported, "The board approved forgiveness, and the vote was seven to five." We laughed.

Yet I can make forgiveness just that calculated, and miss the spontaneous, genuine experience of the heart. I can vote in my head to forgive, but never relinquish the hurt. "If you will just relinquish the need to defend your point of view, you will in that relinquishment gain access to enormous amounts of energy that have been previously wasted," Deepak Chopra writes in *The Seven Spiritual Laws of Success.*

> I have pondered how even the most trivial experience has spiritual potential: any practice that transforms annoyance at self or others into a gift is a form of active mysticism.

News reporter Daniel Schorr tells of coming back to the United States in the 1960s after being in Europe. Media stars already had the big assignments. So he said, "Let me cover the things which your stars are not covering." But almost overnight, what had been leftovers became front-page news: civil rights, poverty, and the environment. Schorr's rise to fame was not without obstacles, however. While reading President Nixon's enemies list on the air, he got to number seventeen and read his own name!

If you can keep yourself free from irritation, negative barriers can emerge as bridges to your life mission.

Rebbe Nachman of Breslov taught that "all barriers and obstacles which confront a person have only one purpose: to heighten one's yearning for the holy deed which the person needs to accomplish. It is part of human nature that the greater the barriers standing in the way of a certain goal, the more one desires to achieve it."

THE FLOWER AND THE GARBAGE: REDEEMING WASTED EXPERIENCES

Here is a silly minimystery of transformation. I am always spilling things—food, drinks, paint, dirt, you name it. One of my daughters does it too. But everyone comes to us to clean out stains! (Peanut butter takes off chewing gum and sticky price tags.) A simple analogy, I admit. But in miniature it speaks a deep truth of human life: that practice even with little irritations leads to clues for conversion of big ones as gifts to the community.

Witnessing the daily devastation caused by napalm and landmines to Vietnamese children and civilians in the 1960s, Thich Nhat Hanh founded and directed the Buddhist School for Youth Social Service in Saigon. Clearly he has spent a lot of time pondering how disciples of the Lord of Love could perpetrate violence. In 1961–62, Nhat Hanh studied at Princeton Theological Seminary. One detects his deep integration of Christian perspectives in his book *Living Buddha, Living Christ* and his recent work *Anger*. Speaking at a conference in the United States, he said: "Nothing in life is wasted. Without garbage we could not have flowers. If the flower is on the way to the garbage, the garbage is on the way to the flower. Every time we see a flower we are not too attached to it: it is on the way to the garbage."

Nhat Hanh draws gentle laughter from his audience when he talks about garbage. He likens human love to the flower cycle: "Our anger must change to compassion and understanding. If we take good care of our present moments, we will take good care of our future." This sounds strangely like Jesus' words: "Do not worry about tomorrow. . . . Consider the lilies of the field. . . ."

Jesus is crucified on Golgotha, the town garbage heap. A Buddhist scripture says, "As a sweet-smelling, lovely lotus may grow upon a heap of rubbish thrown by the highway," so the disciple of the Enlightened One shines in the world. Even wasted experiences, if we meditate on them in the present, can be redeemed.

> By embracing the enlightened One in yourself, you will embrace the wounds in your neighbor; by embracing the crucified One in your neighbor, you will embrace the wisdom in yourself.

Next we explore how rejection is mysteriously transformed into the beauty of art in the lives of artists such as Johann Sebastian Bach and Vincent van Gogh. Then (in Chapter Seventeen) we explore how rejection is mysteriously transformed into the art of political gesture, as exemplified by Mohandas Gandhi and Rosa Parks. Beauty throws a curve ball, and gesture catches it.

Reflection Exercise 24. "Let It Be"

Listen to the Beatles' song "Let It Be" (on the CD *Let It Be*). The title is taken from Mary's words responding to the angel Gabriel's announcement that she would bear a child, which she believed was impossible. Her response was, "Here am I. . . . Let it be to me according to your word" (Luke 1:38). As you hear the words "let it be," or repeat them in your mind, imagine letting go of some past issue that cannot be changed, or accepting some future challenge that may want to birth itself in you. (Capitol Records, Inc., U.S.A.; sound recording by EMI Records Ltd., England, 1970)

Reflection Exercise 25. Let Your Anger Take a Form of Nature

Here is an idea from Flora Slossen Weullner in her book *Heart of Healing, Heart of Prayer*. Sit with your anger and see if it might take some form of nature: a bird, animal, waterfall, or fire. This example shows some male-female differences. Two persons sat in silence. The woman then reported seeing her anger as a wave in the sea, rising to a crescendo and crashing . . . carrying her feelings into the sea of God's love. In the same moment, the man had pictured his anger as a bolt of lightning, zooming red-hot feelings into the cosmic heart of God. (I sometimes picture my anger as a grain of sand, irritating the oyster—and then transforming to a pearl.) See what emerges for you. Reflect on it; draw it in your journal. Share it with someone.

16

BEAUTY

Johann, Vincent, and Jazz

Blackberry winter: the time when the hoarfrost lies on the blackberry blossoms; without this frost the berries will not set. It is the forerunner of a rich harvest.
—MARGARET MEAD, BLACKBERRY WINTER

The role of art is to express the triumph of the human spirit over the mundane and material.
—JOHN BIGGERS, AFRICAN AMERICAN ARTIST

Returning home from two months of fun at the Carlstadt spas in Bohemia, Johann Sebastian Bach was greeted by a black wreath on his door. His wife, Barbara, was dead and buried.

He would always carry the indelible imprint of her sitting upright in their bed the night their twins were born —cradling a tiny baby in each arm. You can sense Bach's suffering in the violin partitas and cello suites he wrote soon afterward, especially in the *Fifth Cello Suite*. "You hear in it," says cellist Yo-Yo Ma, "the

> The mysterious chaos of Bach's life is still creating beauty.

process you go through when you know you have to give up what's most precious."

BACH'S BEAUTY: LIFE OUT OF DEATH

Death was Bach's constant companion. Orphaned at the age of ten and widowed at thirty-five, he saw thirteen of his twenty children die, including a rebellious twenty-four-year-old son.

Death of his life's dreams was an equal companion. The upstart Sebastian was too worldly for the religious and too religious for the worldly. Whether composing for a duke or a parish pastor, he made it a habit to use his rejections to birth him into new arenas. In Mühlhausen, the Pietists attacked him: "This—what is it you call it—counterpoint? Shocking! . . . From the Gospel of John? No one could tell. . . . How can we worship when there are so many different words running together? . . . Art is worldly, too attractive, bound to draw men away from concern for the purity and safety of their souls."

Bach loved wine and a good time with the company of music makers, whether believers or not. When Duke Wilhelm began controlling Bach's friendships, the composer balked. Wilhelm threw him into jail.

Near the end, Bach's supporters dwindled to a handful of academics. His older sons rebelled. When his rector demanded that a mediocre musician would direct his *Kapelle,* the church orchestra, Bach lost his temper, exploding in shouts and blows during a church service. He resigned and retired.

How could he have fallen into such shame? He asked rhetorically, "What is the cause of all such woes?" and answered himself with the words "All my sins have felled Thee" in the *St. Matthew Passion.* Even in his near blindness, he kept writing into the depths of his own sense of failure and exuding beauty. Longing to die, he wrote *Kom suß Tod,* "Come Sweet Death."

Questioning if he had pursued the wrong vision, he tried yet another form, the Mass. Who can help being moved by the

"Crucifixus" of the *Mass in B Minor:* the Man of Sorrows low-ered into the grave, every voice descending into death, and then, the explosion of resurrection?

VAN GOGH'S BROKEN BEAUTY

The life of Vincent van Gogh provides not mere inklings but a veritable flood of transforming mystery. But van Gogh's exquisite art emerged out of the church's rejection of his min-istry among the poor coalminers, and a life of continual rejec-tion.

Growing up in the Netherlands as a pastor's son, Vincent's mystical experience of Christ led him away from his father's established Reformed church to study in what today would be called a Bible college in London. Vincent felt his mission was too urgent for formal theological education. Church officials refused to ordain him; he told them poor miners' families did not need Latin, Hebrew, and Greek. Rather, what they needed was food and clothing to make any sense of God's love. When wealthy urban churches refused even his requests for emergency food supplies, it was the last straw. He left the church, but, as he said, never his Lord.

> Van Gogh's portraiture prefigured our own primodern era: he painted people with an aura of the eternal, which the halo had symbolized in past times. In van Gogh's portraits, light radiates from *within* the faces instead of *above* them.

Living in the pain of failed relationships, alcoholism, poverty, and depression, only his brother Theo continued to believe in him. He wrote of his manic and depressive personal-ity, "The weakness increases from generation to generation." Current geneticists now say this may be true. Van Gogh speaks in his journal of his loneliness: "One may have a blazing hearth in one's soul and yet no one ever comes to sit by it. Passersby see only a wisp of smoke from the chimney and continue on the way."

Vincent would never taste human fame or fortune in his lifetime, yet he expressed the palpable divine glory in his "Sunflowers" and in the "Irises" just outside his room in a mental hospital, during one of his bouts with depression.

Nature, like his life, bade Vincent to contemplate its exquisite beauty and incredible sadness. The cypress came to express life's darkness in counterpoint to the sunflowers, as he explained to his brother Theo: "You need a certain dose of inspiration, a ray from above which is not ours, to do the beautiful things. When I had done these sunflowers, I looked for the contrary and yet the equivalent, and I said this is the cypress. . . . It is as beautiful as the Egyptian obelisk."

In 1889, less than a year before his death, he painted his masterpiece, "Starry Night." The top of the deep green cypress with its fiery streaks flares into the huge stars and planets—the sun and moon overlapping. The village homes and the sky above are ablaze with the light of eternity, but the windows of the village church with its Dutch architecture are dark, symbolizing the unenlightened church leaders who forced him to leave the ministry in 1880, leaving him embittered and alone. Today some of us are called to put the lights back on in the churches; all are called to see the Light beyond institutional walls.

JAZZ: AN EXAMPLE OF PRIMODERN FAITH AND LEADERSHIP

Red Auerbach, former coach of the Boston Celtics, said, "Music washes away from the soul the dust of everyday life." Music provides "a morphology of human senses," to use Suzanne Langer's rich phrase in *Philosophy in a New Key*. Music embodies the form of life itself. As with Bach, music acts as a therapeutic filter for life's polluted waters.

The origin of jazz especially illustrates the upside-down mystery at the heart of existence. Jazz was born out of violence, as white captors stripped away black slaves' African instruments and rhythms. The house slaves were "whitened," European style—acculturating new musical forms and rhythms. Voila! But acculturation works both ways. In the safety of their cabins at night, slaves reverted to their native rhythms, blended with strange new instruments and meter. The very word *blues* comes from the Elizabethan term "blue devils," meaning low spirits. Blues gives jazz its energy and passion. There would be no jazz without blues, and no rock without jazz.

Music can also capture the ecstasy of life, as when we are enraptured in a concert: "Music heard so deeply / That it is not heard at all, but you are the music / while the music lasts," wrote T. S. Eliot. It is no accident that Hebrew Psalms and music "married" each other; both can express mirth or despair. African American spirituals embody these opposites. If you cannot get rid of tragedy, music can alter its effects on your body and brain by making bits of meaning and beauty out of it.

An African American Gospel singer expressed it this way: "I do my best singing when I'm really burdened down." It is Maya Angelou's message: *I Know Why the Caged Bird Sings.* "My grace is sufficient for you, for my power is made perfect in weakness," writes the apostle Paul, for whom the dying-rising One represents "the mystery hidden for ages," changing the raw material of human existence into inklings of beauty and hope.

In the PBS film *Jazz,* produced and directed by Ken Burns, musician Dave Brubeck reminisces about the first black man he ever met—a friend of his father's in California—who bore the scar of a brand on his chest. Brubeck breaks down and cries as he recalls his father saying, "These things can't happen." The experience of turning toward another's pain came like a profound shaft of light, affecting Brubeck's life and vocation. Later, after playing for troops on the European front during World War II with his integrated Wolfpack Band, Brubeck tells of the pain of returning to Texas only to find his African American bandmates were refused service in restaurants. His refusal to eat in white-only establishments authenticated his music. Brubeck is an example of embodied leadership, what Christians mean by incarnation, akin to what Hindus mean by an *avatar.*

JAZZ LEADERSHIP

Jazz provides a model for primodern leadership. The Jewish kabalistic concept of *zimzum* expresses the movement of the Creator stepping back to leave space for the creatures. I have watched close up as Brubeck steps back empty-handed; his countenance brightens; he revels as each player "solos" and assumes leadership.

A leader can inflict evil by failing to step back and listen to the community's context, as Barbara Kingsolver illustrates in *The Poisonwood Bible.* Every Sunday, a missionary preacher in the Congo would end his sermon with: "Tata Jesus is Bangala!" *Bangala* in Kikongo means something precious or dear. But the way the white preacher mispronounced it meant the dreaded "poisonwood tree": "Jesus will make you itch like crazy!" All his life, he never understood even this one basic contradiction, which mirrored his entire abusive mission enterprise and family relationships.

Jazz embodies two gospel truths. The first is the mystery of faith: that even violent stripping away of parts of the self can give rise to a new and beautiful thing. Second is a jazz model of leadership: that love creates by withdrawing, *zimzum,* inviting others into the creative drama.

Reflection Exercise 26. Meditating on Bach's *Mass in B Minor*

Find and listen to the "Crucifixus" from Bach's *Mass in B Minor.* Experience the feelings. Then contrast the feelings of "Et Resurrexit." Note that you are actually hearing parts of the

Apostles' Creed. How does *experiencing* these aspects of a creed with your whole body seem different from saying a creed? Do you sense connections to any "crucifying" and "resurrecting" moments in your own life? Reflect in your journal.

Reflection Exercise 27. Contemplating van Gogh's "Starry Night"

Find a reproduction of Vincent van Gogh's "Starry Night." Contemplate the mysterious obelisk symbol of the cypress tree . . . the overlapping moon and sun . . . the blazing stars, the dark windows of the church. . . . Track down Don McLean's recording of "Starry, Starry Night"; listen while meditating on the painting. Log your responses in your journal.

Reflection Exercise 28. Meditating on Coltrane's *A Love Supreme*

Listen to the jazz CD *A Love Supreme/John Coltrane.* Note how the beat gets in your head first; words are sung only a few times. Contrast *A Love Supreme* with the image of "Almighty God." (*El Shaddai* in Hebrew really means "All-sufficient one.") An option: experience the African American gift of jazz by reading *Duke Ellington: A Spiritual Biography,* by Janna Tull Steed.

17

GESTURE

Gandhi, Rosa, and Soulforce

You must be the change you wish to see in the world.
—MOHANDAS GANDHI

Gesture embraces all. Words are merely the tips of the
icebergs.
—JOAN LIPSCOMB SOLOMON

There is beauty and there are the humiliated. Whatever
difficulties the enterprise may present, I would like never to
be unfaithful to the one or the other.
—ALBERT CAMUS

Visions of political peace can literally kill the dreamer, as
in the case of Gandhi, King, Malcolm X, and Jesus—or
wound the dreamer's inner psyche, as we saw in the life
of formerly exiled Guatemalan poet Julia Esquivel (Chapter
Nine). So Camus could speak of the close connection between
beauty and the humiliated, and his desire to be faithful to both.

The art of beauty serves the art of politics for the good of
the *polis,* the community. The tiny country of Latvia is used to
being invaded, with little chance of fighting back. Said one

Latvian, "We have learned to fight arms with art." Yoko Ono's life embodies art for peace, as did her martyred husband, John Lennon.

Jesus defended the woman who anointed him with costly ointment just before his crucifixion, "Why do you trouble the woman? She has done a beautiful thing to me." Suffering becomes redemptive when something beautiful, true, and good rises within it.

This is why so many artists are society's prophets. This is why books, art, and ideas are banned. The Greeks knew well the interconnection of the good, the beautiful, and the true. Like Bach or van Gogh, Nelson Mandela or Maya Angelou, the wound of rejection can be transformed into a gift for the community. The mystery is in the risings.

GANDHI: FAILED ATTORNEY

When two people complained to me of tiredness in the space of two days, I found myself mentioning the French expression when an artisan gets tired or hurt: "It is the trade entering his body." At times we can absorb societal pain, as in this incident from the life of Mohandas Gandhi.

Returning to India from law school in England, Gandhi seemed unable to relate to the people of India. What could the awkward Mohandas do? Friends and family proposed he go to South Africa, where many Indian citizens lived as exiles, classified as colored.

Later asked what his most meaningful experience was, Gandhi told of a trip in South Africa from Durban to Marowitz, where on arrival a white man entered the train. Gandhi was told he must leave. Calmly, he stated he had ridden first-class from Durban, showed his ticket, and told the officials they would have to remove him by force. This they proceeded to do. In the mountainous night air and subfreezing temperatures, humiliated and separated from his luggage and clothing,

Gandhi became intimate with all the oppressed peoples of the whole world. The trade had entered his body.

This unexpected, mortifying experience would give birth to Gandhi's concept of *Satyagraha*, or "soulforce," combining two Sanskrit words to denote truth and force.

ROSA PARKS AND THE BACK OF THE BUS

You do not have to be famous to incarnate the energy of non-violent truth. When Rosa Parks refused to give up her bus seat to a white man in Montgomery, Alabama, on Thursday, December 1, 1955, she had no intention of getting arrested. She says, "If I had been paying attention, I wouldn't even have gotten on that bus."

For ten years, she had tried to avoid a particular driver who once threw her off a bus on her way to register to vote in 1945. That time, people were crowded into the back stepwell where she was supposed to enter, so she had to walk inside from the front to get to the back. The driver had ordered her off. Fearing for her life, she complied.

In 1955, she found herself unintentionally with this same driver. This time her offense was to sit in a vacant seat in the front of the black section, just behind the whites in the front section. At the next stop, more whites boarded, and the driver announced, "Let me have those front seats." Parks recalls, "As I sat there, I tried not to think about what might happen. I knew that anything was possible. I could be manhandled or beaten. I could be arrested. People have asked me if it occurred to me then that I could be the test case the NAACP had been looking for. I did not think about that at all. In fact if I had let myself think too deeply about what might happen to me, I might have gotten off the bus. I chose to remain."

She was arrested and taken to jail. In the weeks that followed, Parks had to be persuaded by church and community gatherings to allow her experience to become a test case in court.

Parks's one gesture resulted in a bus boycott that birthed the civil rights movement. Genuine spiritual experiences have this quality of serendipity and a kind of reluctance on the part of the participant. That is how you know it is a genuine call.

THE POWER OF GESTURE

In Victor Hugo's *Les Miserables,* Jean Valjean is put in jail for stealing a loaf of bread. Watching the movie or the show *Les Miz,* we sympathize and then celebrate when Valjean is released to the care of a good bishop. But during the night he steals the bishop's best silver and runs. Later, three gendarmes collar the guilty Valjean and bring him to the bishop's door. "Ah, there you are!" said the bishop, looking right at Valjean, "I am glad to see you.

> Gestures have power to bless a person into heaven on earth, or send a person into a living hell. In a first and fearful return to church in two decades, a depressed woman I know tells how if one person had angled a shoulder the wrong way away from her, it would have sent her to suicide.

But! I gave you these candlesticks too. . . ."

The gendarmes are disarmed. They set their captive free and leave. "My friend," said the bishop, "before you go away, here are your candlesticks; take them. . . . Go in peace." He asks only one thing of Valjean: to use the silver to become a genuine human being. When have you received or extended such a gesture of unconditional grace?

> What would it mean to kiss the leper, like St. Francis?

On the other hand, a finger-pointing gesture can cancel out any grace in the speaker's words. A young adult told me he could not pray the Eastern Orthodox "prayer of the heart" ("Lord Jesus Christ have mercy on me") because his mother used to shake her finger if he displeased her: "Jesus'll get you for that."

Honest guilt can awaken a person to love, but unhealthy religion shuts a person down. Worse yet, it triggers the deepest guilt, not just for a wrong thing done but shame for merely being. In subtle ways, we reinforce others' shame. The proverb "giving without receiving is always a downward gesture" has been the bane of much Western charity. Hospitality is mutual giving and receiving. Genuine inter-faith sharing means that both parties risk being changed in the encounter.

Gestures of hospitality represent embodied love. The word becomes flesh; one becomes an avatar, an incarnation of Vishnu in Hindu tradition, like a *bodhisattva* of Buddhist tradition. Luther called it "being a Christ to one's neighbor," an angel unawares, an agent of compassion in a time of need. Gandhi summarized this mystery: "You must be the change you wish to see in the world." Your life becomes the parable; you *are* the gesture.

Reflection Exercise 29. Watching the Movie *Gandhi*

Rent the movie *Gandhi*. Watch for key turning points, gestures, and memorizable phrases. How do you account for Gandhi's sense of resilience in the face of opposition? What can you apply to your life and communities? How did Gandhi's life embody his teaching? What are the risks in following Gandhi's methods?

Reflection Exercise 30. Meditating with *Les Miz*

See the show or rent a video of *Les Miz*, or an older film version of *Les Miserables*, or read the book. Focus on the scene when the good bishop hands Jean Valjean the candlesticks the young man has just stolen from the bishop. Notice your feelings; converse with others. Can you recall ever receiving—or extending—such a gesture of unconditional grace?

18

EMPTINESS
Prozac Days and Dark Nights

As the ancient [Hindu] Rig Veda aphoristically puts it, "
sacrifice is the navel of the universe. . . ." The Jewish
kabbalistic understanding of *zimsum* and the Christian
understanding of the self-emptying God in Christ *(kenosis)*
reflect the crucial significance of the sacrificial dimension
. . . in God's continuing act of creation.
—K. M. GEORGE, THE SILENT ROOTS

Christ was in the world *incognito* and that was His *kenosis.*
—RUSSIAN PHILOSOPHER NICHOLAS BERDYAEV

Sad faces sell things. In a recent "Fashions for the Times"
supplement to the *New York Times Magazine,* I counted on
my fingers and toes the number of happy faces that
advertise "new" fashions in its massive 238 pages. A few others
belie a cynical hint of a smile. Nearly all the rest portray young
and old with sad eyes and drooped lips. In an article, "Puttin' on
le Dog," the poodles look happier than the people.

In the early 1980s, my nephew, who as a teen spent his
summers with us after my brother died, would turn up the radio
to hear Elton John's "Sad Songs" that say so much. I just heard

"Sad Songs" again in a local pharmacy. It left me thinking how one can be sad without being depressed. But no one is depressed, mildly or acutely, without enduring a time of intense sadness.

YOUNG AND BIPOLAR: DEPRESSION IN NEW CLOTHES

In this chapter, I choose to focus on depression and its relationship to spiritual emptiness and the dark night of the soul. First, no one escapes depression's shadow, directly or indirectly: it afflicts huge proportions of those who deal with any kind of loss—jobs, relationships, health, or the ability to live independently—and it affects countless others around them. Second, I speak from experience that the taboo against emotional (in contrast to physical) illness in religious communities leaves masses of spiritual folks painfully orphaned: "If you have faith, you will be happy." Third, the concept of spiritual emptiness (and its cousin the dark night), though not identical with depression, offers room for medical forms of treatment but also brings a unique spiritual perspective to this increasingly devastating social pain.

The diagnosis of bipolar disorder, manic depression's new name, is exponentially on the rise among younger generations. Creative people have always known depression's ambiguous blessings. Our tragic romantic personalities enable us to dream the impossible, but also to catapult us into dark holes. Among the flood of ads for Prozac-type medications is one that highlights van Gogh's portrait. The implication: now not only do masses of folks suffer depression, but they too can be creative geniuses!

Medication can keep a person from going over the edge, as I myself can testify. But ah, would that depression's cure were so simple as a new pill. What about the social matrix contributing to this runaway cultural plague? Meanwhile huge numbers of children grow up to swell the ranks of adults who struggle with this crazy mystery.

BEFRIENDING EMPTINESS: VARIED TRADITIONS

What will the world look like in 2050? or one decade from now? or during the time you read this? I am writing as if at any moment many of us may be emptied of some of our creature comforts. Genuine spirituality means learning to respond, rather than react, to life's diminishments in such a way as to find an invitation.

All spiritual traditions have some concept of emptiness. It is an aspect of the Hebrew Sabbath: to cease, to shut down our internal computers. If we fail to claim healthy soul space, life will hand us sabbath in the form of a car crash or a curve ball, a divorce or depression, a debilitating illness or vocational crisis.

Spiritual practices of East and West would tell us, Do not wait for life to empty you. Learn to befriend emp-tiness as a rich source of creativity and courage. The many books about emptiness remind me of subtle distinctions in its Eastern and Western concepts. Even so, I am convinced that within these varied concepts lies an overlapping center of spiritual experience of emptiness that produces a common fruit of compassion, as we now explore.

> Here is the mystery: if we look into our empty faces we may find our treasure in the burned-out places of our lives, until, phoenixlike, the dark spaces become the next egg of creativity.

The Hebrew Bible's opening lines in Genesis read: "The earth was a formless void, and darkness covered the face of the deep"—just before the big bang when light exploded. Voilà! The Life Force spoke (or vibrated): "Let there be light!"

The idea of a necessary void preceding new life lies at the heart of the kabalistic mystical tradition of Judaism. As we have seen, *zimzum* refers to the Creator "stepping back," like the jazz conductor, to make room for the creatures. This stepping back allows for *ein sof,* creative emptiness where something comes out of nothing. The Jewish idea of *zimzum* and the Christian idea of the self-emptying God in Christ *(kenosis)* dramatize the crucial sacrificial aspect of God's ongoing creativity.

The V-shaped pattern in the diagram that follows represents three classic movements: the crisis of withdrawal, the void or abyss, and the return to union with all created things.

The New Testament urges disciples to practice the mind-set of Christ Jesus, who emptied *(kenosis* in Greek) himself to the point of death, even though he was equal to God, according to Paul in Philippians 2.

The Buddhist experience of *Sunyata* as emptiness and the *ein sof* of the Jewish Kabala draw Christians back to our own truth: the self-emptying *kenosis* of Christ is not only an event in history or a belief in our head, but a mind-set of the heart, a moment-by-moment experience in one's own history.

This inner mind-set of emptiness is countercultural. It sounds very Eastern but it marks the character of every true disciple. For Christians, *kenosis* means living out one's baptism, dying and rising in Christ. It means personal and political resiliency, as in the Egyptian death and resurrection myth of Isis and Osiris. It means letting go of one's own preconceived ideas—whether of self-inflation or self-deprecation—and then opening oneself to amazing possibilities.

It is a movement from the demon of controlling (or being controlled) to freedom; from "What do *I* want to do with my life?" (or, for many women and minorities, from "What do *others* want to do with my life?") to "What is Life inviting me to become?"

In *Spiritual Emptiness,* Donald W. Mitchell draws on a Buddhist Christian poetic image of the void, comparing the deep "Golgothan hole" of Jesus' cross with the womb of the Buddha's enlightenment at the Bodhi tree. For the Christian,

Kenosis, Ein Sof, Sunyata: Emptying Preconceived Attitudes, Plans, and Ideas

"Love leaves its high holy temple."
–Maya Angelou

"The capacity of the mind is as great as that of space."
–Buddhism, Sutra of Hui Neng 2

"The Tao is like the bellows: it is empty yet infinitely capable."
–Lao Tzu

"Let the same mind be in you that was in Christ Jesus,
who though he in the form of God . . . emptied himself."
–Philippians 2:5–7

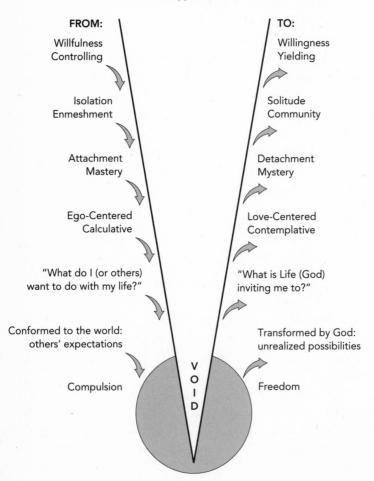

FROM:	TO:
Willfulness Controlling	Willingness Yielding
Isolation Enmeshment	Solitude Community
Attachment Mastery	Detachment Mystery
Ego-Centered Calculative	Love-Centered Contemplative
"What do I (or others) want to do with my life?"	"What is Life (God) inviting me to?"
Conformed to the world: others' expectations	Transformed by God: unrealized possibilities
Compulsion	Freedom

VOID

the Golgothan hole of emptiness is not an end in itself; nor is the womb for the Buddhist. For each, the empty space is the birthing place of compassionate living for others.

EVERYDAY PRACTICE OF *KENOSIS*

In a best-selling Dr. Seuss book, *Oh, The Places You'll Go,* Theodore Geisel describes the *kenosis* process:

> You will come to a place where the streets are not marked.
> Some windows are lighted. But mostly they're darked. . . .
> You can get so confused
> that you'll start in to race
> down long wiggled roads at a break-necking pace
> and grind on for miles across weirdish wild space,
> headed, I fear, toward a most useless place.
>
> The Waiting Place . . .

Our normal way of viewing things is to "get so confused" when Murphy's Law operates full-time: everything that can possibly go wrong goes wrong. Instead, imagine the "most useless place" as a womb: What if the difficulties happen to divert us from the intensity of some big thing that wants to be born, so it can be born as beautifully as possible?

"Wait, I think we have touched something very important here. Let's not talk about it. Let's wait for two weeks, and let it solve itself." Thus Werner Heisenberg, the Nobel Prize winner famous for his uncertainty principle of quantum physics, would speak to his researcher in the middle of some problem. "Colorless green ideas sleep furiously," wrote Noam Chomsky; that is, powerful insights gestate unawares; do not wake them too soon.

Maya Angelou's poetry gushed forth only after a prolonged period of self-chosen silence. Great works of art gestate in a void of silence. We are sometimes literally dumbfounded, speechless for brief moments or long periods, like Isaiah after the king died, or Zechariah after hearing a birth announcement. The two words call us back to the true self: *dumb* speaks of our being silenced, emptied (*kenosis, ein sof, Sunyata*). *Founded* speaks of a new plane of existence, a new foundation for our life.

DARK NIGHT AS SPIRITUAL TRANSFORMATION

Plotinus, Denys, and Gregory of Nyssa in the early church spoke of the abyss of God's love as a "dark ray," which we now know scientifically as black light.

A prolonged period of *kenosis* can become a dark night of the soul. *Dark* speaks of destruction, disaster, death, disintegration. *Night* conveys newness, nearness, intimacy, transformation. Taken together, a *dark night* experience can transform the harsh diminishments of life into a thing of depth and beauty. It has a long history.

"Moses entered the thick darkness where God was," says the Torah in Exodus 20. Right after receiving light in the Ten Commandments, Moses enters the dark *via negativa,* hiding out in the shadow of the divine wing, close but unable to see directly.

Nicodemus came to see Jesus by night, when Jesus told him "You must be born anew." The apostle Paul, after encountering Christ, retreated at once to Arabia, and then to Syria. Only after a three-year blackout period did Paul contact the establishment church in Jerusalem.

Like the apostle Paul, Abu Hamid al-Ghazzali, a prominent Muslim theologian, underwent a spiritual breakdown in the late eleventh century: "I have poked into every dark recess, I have made an assault on every problem, I have plunged into every abyss. . . . God shriveled my tongue. . . ." Al-Ghazzali left his professorship in Baghdad and retreated for several years. He found his faith renewed by engaging in Sufi-like practices. He returned as a great Sufi voice for uniting reason and mystical experience.

The dark night is especially linked with the fifteenth-century Spanish mystic John of the Cross, whose childhood poverty contained a seed of his suffering and genius. Young John worked in a hospital and went to school by day. He would study late into the night. Thus as a youth John had already made night his friend.

At times, the night can arrive with no outward crisis. This night corresponds to the abyss in mysticism and is akin to chaos theory in science and disintegration in psychological literature. In *Sacred Sorrows: Embracing and Transforming Depression,* Andrea Nelson speaks of disintegrating to new life in her essay "Chaos Theory and Depression": "The new tools of Chaos mathematics reveal patterns of order deeply embedded in the tempest seething around us. It rekindles an ancient idea of creative tension between order and chaos that dates to early Greek philosophers and to diverse creation myths that invoke a primordial state of chaos from which all things spring forth. . . . The Greek roots of the word *chaos* convey a sense of an empty space or abyss—a formlessness that contains the seeds of creativity."

"All things ceased; I went out from myself," wrote John of the Cross. Sometimes the abyss seems like a night that never ends, sometimes like a winter that will not go away. Camus wrote, "In the depth of winter, I finally learned that there lay within me an invincible summer."

DEPRESSION AND DARK NIGHT

A student asked her therapist, "What would be the difference between depression and the dark night?" The counselor paused and then answered: "The outcome." For some, depression ends in burnout and bitterness. For others, it is a brief stage: lose a job, get a new one. For still others, it leads to transformation;

you begin to ask, "What do I have a job *for?*" The same experience becomes a spiritual night to open the depth of Life. The key is in how one responds.

"Depression is the flaw in love. To be creatures who love, we must be creatures who can despair at what we lose, and depression is the mechanism of that despair," writes Andrew Solomon in *The Noonday Demon: An Atlas of Depression*. F. Scott Fitzgerald wrote in *The Crack-Up* that "in a real dark night of the soul it is always three o'clock in the morning, day after day." Those night demons have visited me.

Night Demons

They come in the night,
these demons of self-doubt—
they come to disqualify me,
kidnapping my confidence:
How can you be spiritual
yet be this anxious?
How dare you offer
your needy self to be
a spiritual guide for others?

Then the Spirit comes—
to comfort, to console,
fortifying me with
the ancient assurance
that I am one beggar
showing other beggars
where to find bread,
that my very neediness
validates my credentials,
as one who surely seeks
and just as surely finds,
—as one already found.

Once, as I was all ready to lead a seminar, a physician asked, "What do you think really happened on Easter?" I confessed not knowing in *fact* what happened to Jesus' physical body. Nevertheless, for me the empty tomb stories in the Gospels are *real*. It is women, like Mary Magdalene (my intuitive self), who have the courage to go to the tomb and confront its dark emptiness. When Mary tells the men (my practical self), they go back to fishing. But she stays and weeps. I, too, have leaned into the empty tomb, sure that my Lord was taken away. Then, as sad and scared as Mary, I turn outward to see Jesus anonymously, *incognito,* in the face of the gardener—in the world, in the ordinary place, in the least of these. That, I said, is what I mean by journeying alongside the Jesus of history to the Christ of experience. Jesus keeps showing up, but what if I don't speak to the gardener?

MEDICAL TREATMENT AND SPIRITUAL TRANSFORMATION

Driving back home from lunch one day, I confided in a trusted colleague, "Art, I'm sorry I wasn't a very good conversationalist today—this is one of my down times." He jibed, "I like you better this way!" When I am not so full of myself, there is more space to listen.

"The opposite of depression is not happiness but vitality, and my life, as I write this, is vital, even when sad," concludes Andrew Solomon in *The Noonday Demon.* "Every day, I choose, sometimes gamely and sometimes against the moment's reason, to be alive. Is that not a rare joy?"

Emotional illness, whether mild or major, may become an occasion for deepening spiritual life and love. If insulin for diabetes or psychotherapy for depression can free a person to follow love's call, that too is the Spirit's work. Like diabetes, if mental illness requires medical treatment, use it. Or as with a broken leg, use crutches until it heals.

But unlike diabetes or a broken bone, because of the shame our culture projects on those of us who suffer emotional pain, I believe a spiritual lens on this goofy gory gift is not a luxury, but essential to staying vital—even when you feel sad or others think you are wacko.

If you're on crutches or insulin or Prozac, you can still meet with a spiritual companion or counselor to talk about patterns of meaning in your journey and where life is leading you. That can color blah prosaic days with nighttime's mysterious intimacy.

I pray for the masses of youth and their elders to celebrate inklings of spiritual vitality, even within their sadness. The mystery of death and rebirth goes on everywhere. The world is filled with bits and pieces of Eucharist.

Reflection Exercise 31. Meditating on McKennitt's "Dark Night"

Listen to Loreena McKennitt as she sings the poem by John of the Cross, "The Dark Night of the Soul," on her CD *The Mask and the Mirror* (Warner Bros. Records, 1994). What experiences or feelings does John's classic poem surface for you? Or does it leave you wordless, lost in wonder? An option: read Psalm 139:11–12: "If I say, 'Surely the darkness shall cover me, / and the light around me become night,' / even the darkness is not dark to you; / the night is as bright as the day, for darkness is as light to you."

Reflection Exercise 32. Emptiness as Space for Love

Become aware of some emptiness in your life, an unfulfilled desire you may rarely express. Gently get in touch with it. One somewhat private person said, "It was that my mother died and never got to see my husband and children." It may be a kind of a spiritual homing instinct, "a God-shaped vacuum." Gently look at things you may be using to fill it, or deny it—creative, or destructive. Prayerfully, offer the emptiness by thinking of it as "space for Love."

Reflection Exercise 33. Meditating on a Diminishment, and Gifts

Scan over your life to become aware of some place of diminishment or difficulty—physical, economical, emotional, or vocational. Spend some time pondering: Have any gifts emerged from that experience—personally? or communally? Write in your journal. Find a way to celebrate any gifts.

19

SEX, MYSTICISM, AND WORK

Do I really believe that my life comes to me as a gift and
that there is in me a terrific thing?
—Alan Jones, Exploring Spiritual Direction

Teenagers, then, groping in the back seat of a TransAm
are a latent liturgy, unconscious of the One
for whom they are really on fire.
—W. Paul Jones, hermit, Teaching a Dead Bird to Sing

The soul is generative, like God is.
—Meister Eckhart

Growing up not far from Intercourse, Pennsylvania, even
as a child I enjoyed all the jokes and puns about sex.
Intercourse in original English usage can refer to intimate conversation, but also to working commerce at the inter-
section of main roads. In some such way, the small town in
Lancaster County got its unique name.

Here we have three themes: sex, mystical intimacy, and
work. First we look at the gift of eros, our sexuality, and its
abuses. Then we see how spiritual intimacy echoes our longings

for Love beyond all human loves. Finally we explore how erotic energies are transformed into vocational generativity in the creative commerce of life.

SEXUALITY, THE "TERRIFIC THING"

Sexuality is our divinely given desire for loving, life-giving intimacy that nurtures all areas of life. However, it is often abused and just as often misunderstood only as physical expression.

As sexual values change, we need to speak openly of sex as a "terrific thing," as exhilarating yet frightening as Everest. Sexuality is to be enjoyed and protected, according to each one's sense of calling.

Our erotic energies are integrally related to our deepest longings, sufferings, and joys. Healthy spirituality is all about naming and validating human experiences of joy *and* pain. Only then can our whole selves, broken and blessed, become vessels of Love.

Sexuality is a sacred terrific gift, to be guarded and celebrated: lovingly and responsibly, safely and gently. Sex is not dirty. But when abused or violated, sex can become the source of our greatest pain.

If tomorrow's faith communities are to help restore the passion and compassion of life, we must break the stained-glass silence about the gift and the abuse of sexuality.

But sadly, schools, churches, and businesses often try to silence the hurt and even reward people to be silent, magnifying the pain. Just as institutions are often silent about abuse, they are also silent about the gift of sexuality.

Love means tuning a just ear to orphaned voices of abused women and children, of men or women in dead-end careers, caught between eking out their survival and selling their soul to dehumanizing systems. We must not assume simplistically that silence is always golden.

One reason many fear solitude is because painful memories resurface: of silence used as punishment by family and society.

We can validate isolated souls in personal conversations or public speaking, in classrooms, sanctuaries, and workrooms; just to name briefly the rejection of minorities, silenced women or voiceless children, gay persons or childless couples can begin to transform negative silence into healing space.

Today's sex-saturated culture creates a golden opportunity to break the silence about the gift and the abuse of eros and point directly to spiritual dimensions of sexuality in all of life and work—through film and music, poetry and sports.

SEXUAL SPIRITUAL MYSTICISM

Over dinner I was telling a small group how a lay chaplain conducts a "spiritual life assessment" by asking, "What is your favorite love song?" Answers often reveal clues about a person's image of God. Then one person asked me, "What is *your* favorite love song?" I had never answered it for myself, but then I began singing softly "The Shadow of Your Smile." (My wife and I heard this theme from the film *The Sandpiper* over and over during our honeymoon in 1966.)

"Maria," a haunting song from the musical *West Side Story,* echoes these twin yearnings for sexual and spiritual intimacy: "Maria," as in playing a love song, or as in praying.

There it is: I am more likely to know God indirectly—hiding out in the shadow of the rock, romancing in the soul's night.

To face our homesickness squarely, to embrace our longings rather than fill them with false gods, takes courage. If we stop to listen, our short-lived human desires beckon us home to our deepest Desire.

We are not disembodied spirits. That is a tragic mistake of many gnostic religions in old and new variations, to seek the sacred outside the temple of the body, as if the body is evil or at best irrelevant. Manicheans in the early centuries of the Common Era endorsed a split: body versus soul, light versus dark, good versus evil. The Jewish-Christian idea of resurrection of the body sanctifies the flesh. In nearly all religions, vital faith is compared to romancing with the divine Lover—the ultimate mystical union of the sexual and the spiritual.

A young adult tuned into a Spanish-language radio station in his car. *"Yo quiero mas de ti,"* the singer crooned again and again;"I want more of you." Immediately the phrase gave voice to his longing for God: *"Yo quiero mas de ti."* It has become his mantra, a breath prayer, a prayer of the heart cycling round and round in his fast-paced life.

Like the biblical Song of Songs, John of the Cross uses romantic language to describe spiritual joy. John's poem expresses an experience of genuine love where the self-conscious ego dies:"He wounded my neck / With his gentle hand / Suspending all my senses."

Sexual self-expression in solitude may embody a deep prayerful yearning to commune and intercede with all creation—a longing for loving union with God, neighbor, and self. Such expressions can take the form of gardening or sports, poetry or music, art or altruism.

In acts of self-forgetting love, positive endorphins are released akin to the experience of orgasm. We can experience mystical sexuality in very concrete forms of service: compassion for a rejected person, or passion for a social cause.

WORK AS GENERATIVITY: ORIGINAL BLESSING

"To love and to work": so Freud described twin aspects of human life. In a sex-saturated and economically driven culture, we spend most of our energies on relationships and work. Sex and work are also the two areas of our body's deepest passion and pain. Thus we desperately crave spiritual intimacy beyond our human loves, and spiritual fulfillment beyond our routine work.

> Sex and work are so intimately related because our real work is to express creativity in all of life. This is our *Original Blessing* (to borrow Matthew Fox's book title) and the meaning of his theme of "creation spirituality."

Good news! In the primal Hebrew stories in Genesis, sex and work are originally blessed. In the first Hebrew story of creation (Genesis 1), our bodies are created "in the image of God.... Male and female ... God blessed them." Humankind is given the gift of caring for creation. Each act of creation is pronounced "good," and after creating human beings God declares: "And it was *very* good." In the second story (Genesis 2), Adam and Eve "were naked and were not ashamed." They are placed in the garden "to till it and to keep it," all *before* there is any mention of sin or fall.

Sex and work are created good; there is no "original" sin. However, something happens to our original blessing (Genesis 3): work degenerates into drudgery and sex into exploitation. Society glamorizes sex, but fundamentalist religions subtly reinforce the negative: sex is dirty and work is a curse. This puts our bodies in a real bind. The good news is that both sex and work are redeemed, revalued. But to present your body as a spiritual vessel, you need to begin by being present to it, which is one benefit of these reflection exercises.

> The spiritual message of East and West is that the intensity of sexual passion embodies our deepest spiritual hungers, woundings, and bliss. Even tragic sexual pain can mysteriously be the invitation to seek the divine Lover and holy healing work.

Here is the mystery: How is it that some place of disintegration at the margins can become the place of integration in the center? How is it that rebellion against religion can lead to faith? How is it that the worldly path of sex and work addiction or abuse can turn itself into the spiritual path of self-understanding and vocational generativity?

In the film *The End of the Affair,* based on Graham Greene's novel set in war-torn London in the 1940s, Sarah, a married woman, falls in love with Maurice Bendrix, a cynical novelist. After a turbulent five-year affair, Sarah finds Bendrix pinned by a bomb beneath the front door of their apartment, presuming him dead. In that moment, she makes a deal with a God in whom she does not believe: to give Bendrix up if he is allowed to live. When a few minutes later Bendrix walks into the room alive, Sarah begins her spiritual journey and breaks off with her lover, while railing against God even as she begins to take religious instruction. Gradually she comes to a profound faith and a change of social values.

A sexual crisis may not lead to a direct faith transformation, but it may be subliminally transformed into meaningful and generative work. In the movie *Billy Elliot,* a coalminer's son takes ballet lessons while his father thinks he is training to be a boxer. At one point, another kid asks Billy if his teacher has sex. "No, she's unfulfilled," answers Billy, "that's why she does the dancin'." It is a revealing line.

In her book *Silences,* Tillie Olsen tells painful yet transforming stories of many women and some men whose voices were silenced for years—but were later validated. During a long fast of being silenced, fertile gifts of writing or art can be gestating.

We all knew the open secret of my high school English teacher, Miss Laura Long: her only love died in World War I. She had no children—except thousands of us students. Walking down the aisle, she would gesture, "Now that's what Shakespeare said. But Kent, what is *your* philosophy of life?" I am still living the answer.

Here is a mysterious kind of spiritual sublimation. How many anonymous "nuns and monks" quietly transform disillusioned sexual intimacy into countless ways that create intimate conversations and creative commerce to bless the world?

Reflection Exercise 34. Contemplating Your Favorite Love Song

Take a few minutes to muse: "What is my favorite love song?" Hear it in your head. Or play a recording of it. If you have the skill, play it on an instrument, drum it, or tap it. When did you first hear it? What memories does it spawn? Can you notice romantic spiritual meanings? Note associations in your journal. Find someone to converse with about the experience.

Reflection Exercise 35. Reading the Bible's "Song of Songs"

Poetry is often more expressive when read aloud. Find time (about thirty to sixty minutes) to read the ancient "Song of Songs." Note its sensual images. Create your own inner "Hollywood video," imagining sounds of the turtle dove, images of a gazelle, spiced wine, nursing breasts, and pomegranates. Does any sense of spiritual-mystical connection come to mind as you imagine the lovemaking? Meditate on Chapter 5:1: "I slept, but my heart was awake. / Listen, my beloved is knocking."

Reflection Exercise 36. Meditative Thanks with the Body

Sit in stillness; slow down your breathing. Allow a centering word or image to arise (see Reflection Exercise 10, in Chapter Five). Slowly, using the image or word, inhale lovingly . . . meditate . . . exhale thankfully. . . . Begin with your left foot . . . right foot . . . left ankle . . . etc., each area of the body up through your abdomen . . . to your heart . . . then each shoulder, arm, hand. . . . Return to your larynx . . . parts of the face . . . to the top of your head. . . . Enjoy an aura of peace.

HOW SHALL WE THEN LIVE?

Having Fun Doing Good

We are simply asked to make gentle our bruised world.
To be compassionate of all, including oneself,
Then in the time left over to repeat the ancient tale,
And go the way of God's foolish ones.
—PETER BYRNE

Don't ask yourself what the world needs. Ask yourself what makes
you come alive, and then go do that. Because what the world needs is
people who have come alive.
—HOWARD THURMAN

20

PLAYFUL PROJECTS
FOR SERIOUS
PURPOSES

Whoever welcomes one such child in my name welcomes
me, and whoever welcomes me welcomes not me but the
one who sent me.
—JESUS

Devastating earthquakes were in the news. I was fasci-
nated to hear a report on how rescue dogs are trained
to go into rubble to sniff out humans. It all begins as
play, like hide and seek. Dogs are enticed to go behind certain
trees: find a humanoid, get a reward—no humanoid, no reward.
I recalled a phrase I once heard: "playful projects for serious purposes."

As I told this story later, a woman who is blind spoke up.
Her dog, Jazz, was commissioned to the Ground Zero rescue in
New York City in 2001 and the Oklahoma City bombing site in
1994. She said, "Things got so awful, the dogs grew so discour-
aged, that play sessions had to be scheduled with live persons to
renew the dogs' spirits."

An ancient proverb says that Sabbath is to play and to pray.
The Buddha laughs. Jesus is constantly having fun doing good—
often on the Sabbath—partying, and playing with words as he

tells about parties. Yet it is all for the most serious purpose: the soul's connection with its own Ground, and, like the giant sequoias, with its neighbors' roots bearing support.

HAVING FUN DOING GOOD

Now is the time to let our compass draw us to magnetic north, with its single theme: How shall we then live? It is the question that draws you home, your North Star to discern your direction at night. If you live below some spiritual equator of your life, the question still draws you North, but you must occasionally look behind at night to the Southern Cross for orientation. These next chapters give us a sense of direction by varied degrees and angles of vision.

How shall we then live? So what? Even if we have experienced surprise bits of grace in the grit, or an inkling of transformation, what difference? For a clue, the question leads us to revisit Kierkegaard's four stages along life's way: having fun, doing good, burning out, and coming home (recall the sign for infinity in Chapter Five). I picture these stages as cyclical rather than sequential because we are always returning home again for the first time:

> We shall not cease from exploration
> And the end of all our exploring
> Will be to arrive where we started
> And know the place for the first time.
>   —T. S. ELIOT

Eliot captures the primal image of the wheel from the Hindu Vedic tradition, from Ezekiel and Ecclesiastes for Jewish-Christian believers, from ancient Egypt as the daily rising and setting of the sun god Ra, from Taoism as the yin-yang symbol, and from the early church as a continuous baptismal process of daily dying and rising.

The sign for infinity, with its two elliptically shaped wheels, offers a primodern symbol. These wheels are primal, cycling round without our thinking, connecting us to infinite unconscious wisdom. They are also modern, because when you do think about it, these wheels are going somewhere, like streams that flow into each other. Combining the primal wheels with Kierkegaard's modern existential stages, we can see these stages in the life of the Buddha—and of the prodigal and perfectionist brothers in Jesus' parable (see Chapter Five). We see our own life cycling around.

> When we become too serious, "the way that has power to free us"—the *Tao Te Ching*—is the way of Jesus' playful conundrum: become like a child.

We seekers sometimes begin the spiritual journey by having fun, playing with life—toying around with drugs, sex, money, and even religions and intellectual ideas. Then after the fifth trip to just about anywhere—Cancun, a drug high, the slammer, the meditation center—we decide to try doing good. But pretty soon we feel like a Peace Corps volunteer who said, "All my best efforts were like trying to bail out the Atlantic ocean one leaky thimbleful at a time." Other times, we begin with the dutiful stage of doing good, and only later venture into the wayward stage of having fun, sometimes even in the name of very righteous causes.

> Mysteriously, you begin to cycle through the same stages with a whole new lens of perception. The burning out becomes a burning passion in your heart; you can have fun while doing good, and discover what home really is.

Whether from having too much fun or from doing too much good, we reach the stage of burning out. To begin the journey, or begin again, is to come to oneself, like the prodigal. It means confessing that the awkward things we do to satisfy our longings turn our clumsy path back home again for the first time.

Children
We are children first,
>>> then try feverishly
>>> to become adults,
>>> until painfully
we become children again.
>>> And again. . . .

PURGATION: FROM BURNING OUT TO BURNING PASSION

Most of us cycle back and forth through these stages, looking for a path to integrate our fragmented selves. If we stay with it, somehow the cycling around becomes a form of purgation, preparing our way for wholeness. Cynical cycles are now redeemed.

How can we go the distance, from "do the grunge work, have fun later" to "have fun doing good" at the very same time? Maxim Gorky gives us a clue in his *Autobiography:* "In time I came to understand that out of the misery and murk of their lives the Russian people had learned to make sorrow a diversion, to play with it like a child's toy; seldom are they diffident about showing their happiness. And so, through their tedious weekdays, they made a carnival of grief. . . ."

I can get so serious about the world's needs that all the life is sucked out of me. To go the distance, to make a carnival of grief, I need to spend time contemplating Howard Thurman's wisdom: "Ask yourself what makes you come alive, and then go do that, because what the world needs is people who have come alive."

The pay lies hidden in the play. Hunter "Patch" Adams was criticized in his official medical school record for "excessive happiness." A faculty advisor once yelled, "If you want to be a clown, join the circus." The movie *Patch Adams* is his real story of combining clowning and compassion by founding the Gesundheit Institute, in West Virginia, dedicated to a holistic approach to medicine.

Burned into my early consciousness is the answer to the first question in the Presbyterian "Westminster Catechism": What is the chief end of humanity? *Humanity's chief end is to glorify God and enjoy God forever.* Whatever misshapen sin and guilt was laid on my youthful heart, I still use this like twenty-twenty vision for discerning little and big things: something's not right if I can't experience at least a tad of joy while going through the most difficult places.

Reflection Exercise 37. Revisiting Kierkegaard's Stages

Revisit Kierkegaard's stages along life's way (see the figure in Chapter Five). Contemplate any moments when all four seemed to converge: having fun while doing good with a burning passion in your heart—that really seemed like coming home.

Reflection Exercise 38. Meditating on "Action, Inaction"

"One who sees the inaction that is in action and the action that is in inaction is wise indeed" (Bhagavad Gita, chapter 4:18). It is the idea of *wu-wei* in Zen: action through no action. Ponder this in relation to Jesus' silence before Pilate in the Roman political court: "Pilate asked him, 'What is truth?' . . . Pilate entered his headquarters again and asked Jesus, 'Where are you from?' But Jesus gave him no answer" (John 18:38, 19:9). Notice any time when your own inaction became an active witness to love. An option: listen to "The Sound of Silence" on *The Best of Simon and Garfunkel* (www.sonymusic.com/artists/SimonAndGarfunkel).

21

LIVE AS IF YOU HAD A THOUSAND YEARS TO LIVE, LIVE AS IF YOU MUST DIE TOMORROW

Do not hurry; do not rest.
—GOETHE

The opposite of a true statement is a false statement, but the opposite of a profound truth can be another profound truth.
—NIELS BOHR

Write as if you were dying. . . .
—ANNIE DILLARD, THE WRITING LIFE

How shall we then live? Mother Ann Lee of the Shakers affirmed a living paradox: "Do all your work as if you had a thousand years to live, and as you would if you knew you must die tomorrow." I often ask groups, "What do these words say to you?" Once a woman responded with a profound truth: "Live your life with perspective and passion."

"Go to the head of the class," we said. Everyone wrote it down.

I pondered how history is what gives perspective. The way I was taught, history left me bored. But I have come to see that our own fragmented stories are little histories spliced into a great sweep of history; that gives perspective.

Browsing our family bookshelf, my wife found a little book called *Magic Eye II*. I remember looking at it with our kids in their teens. Each page appears as a plain flat design—some have little birds, others waves of the sea—until you contemplate each one for a time. Then something magic occurs. You see three dimensionally: a whole flock of birds flying over gorgeous mountain heights, waves that take you down into an ocean of brilliant sea creatures! If a page won't focus, just play with it a bit, up close, then farther away. Perspective can create an amazing world of passion beneath life's surface.

PASSION AND PERSPECTIVE— AND ROMERO

How shall we then live? This is *the* big question, one that has haunted me since I heard it and I hope always will. The question guided Francis Schaffer, an evangelical Christian who spent much of his life in Switzerland, where the world's marginalized people were welcome in his home. Even if they burned cigarette holes in the furniture or left the place so it had to be fumigated, they were still welcome.

> You discover the Force of love is already using you, changing you through the bruises and the battles and the funny friendships with people you would not even sip a Coke with a year ago.

How do you pay back if you are fortunate to find even a few flecks of gold in the grit of life, even weeks or years or decades later? The Native American perspective is always to give back: cut a tree, plant a tree. Kill a deer, protect an endangered owl. It is the upside-down perspective of Jesus: "Give, and it shall be given unto you."

How can we live with passion? A decade ago, an African American woman sensed our group's midafternoon lethargy. "I'm going to teach you folks to sing with your bodies," she said. With no printed music or accompaniment, we all began to sway and walk and clap singing, "I'm gonna live so God can use me, I'm gonna live so God can use me . . . anywhere, Lord, anytime." On we went: "I'm gonna pray so. . . . I'm gonna sing so. . . . I'm gonna work so. . . ." Living passionately creates perspective.

Right there I knew the answer to my big question. You do not sit around praying for more faith. You go out and start living *as if* you had faith.

Such is the amazing story of Oscar Romero of El Salvador. The church hierarchy elected him archbishop, sure that he would hold a conservative line, not rock any boats. But Romero's ear turned to God and the poor at the same time. The cries of the "disappeared" and the raped women and orphaned children became for Romero the cry of Jesus abandoned on the cross: "My God, My God, why have you forsaken me?" Going about his job created his passion—and endangered his life. He was assassinated at the communion altar while saying, "This is my body, given for you. . . . This is my blood. . . ." In the movie *Romero,* you can hear the archbishop say shortly before his murder, "If I am killed I will resurrect in the people of El Salvador." That is the thousand-year perspective.

PASSION AND PERSPECTIVE— AND "SECULAR APOSTLES"

You get a feeling sometimes, like Romero, almost against your will or your better judgment, of being *sent*—the meaning of *apostle,* one who is sent. You get sent someplace you did not expect or want to go, or sent somewhere in your thinking that leaves you feeling orphaned with friends who cannot understand. Like Moses, who murdered an Egyptian, or like the shooting star preacher (Robert Duvall) in the movie *Apostle,* you may be running away from something bad. But your flight may turn you into a shooting star, sent into the world to empower others to do foolish things.

I will tell you a secret: I believe there are a lot of secular apostles. Let me describe just a few in the hope that many of us may be inspired to join in their train.

"Can Bono save the world? Don't laugh—the globe's biggest rock star is on a mission to make a difference." There was this headline with the rock star's photo on the cover of *Time.* There were his amazing interviews with conservative Senator Strom Thurmond on "Larry King Live." There was Bono out there advocating for massive investment in AIDS research and help for orphaned children in Africa and everywhere. Living passionately creates perspective: *there* becomes *here* and *then* becomes *now.*

Bruce Springsteen tells how shortly after September 11, 2001, he was pulling out of a beach parking lot in the Jersey Shore town of Sea Bright when a fan rode by. The man rolled down his window and shouted, "We need you!" and drove on. It was the seed for Springsteen's new album, *The Rising.* Ordinary office workers, firefighters, police officers, and air travelers who died on September 11 become heroes in "a song cycle about duty, love, death, mourning, and resurrection...." Despite tragedy, the songs ring "with a recurring hope that there's a way to rise above suffering." A young woman returned from a Springsteen concert in Philadelphia saying she experienced three months of church.

Years after her death, Princess Diana still serves as an icon of beautiful compassion. Her passion for peace, feeding hungry children, and ridding the world of landmines remains a living legacy. As I write this, landmines in the Ukraine are being dismantled and recycled into children's toys for Christmas.

AMAZING GRACE AND SECOND CHANCES

"Amazing Grace" has become an international anthem. Its haunting African rhythms echo in stadiums, churches, inside people's heads. Its composer, John Newton, was a wealthy English slave trader who regularly kidnapped native Africans. Then he was converted to Christ. But what is seldom told is that Newton still engaged in slave trading for years after his conversion—until he had this dream.

Newton saw himself on a sailing ship in Venice, suddenly approached by a stranger who gave him a ring, telling him his life would be full of happiness as long as he had this ring. Delighted with the gift, Newton kept it with him till a friend made fun of him for his superstition. He threw the ring into the sea. Instantly, he saw a great fire on shore and knew he would be drawn into the flame. Regretting deeply that he threw away the ring, he stood looking at where it had sunk into the sea. Suddenly the stranger stood at his side, asking him why he looked so sad. He confessed how he had been given the ring and then stupidly threw it away. The stranger plunged into the sea and then reappeared with the ring. Newton demanded its return, but the stranger replied, "I will keep it for you. But whenever you need the power of the ring, remember I will always be at your side."

At the moment he awoke from the dream, Newton stated, he felt like a piece of wood rescued from the fire. The dream became the turning point. At once he gave up his career of slave trading to become an Anglican priest and work to abolish slavery.

What if he had not paid attention to his dream? What if a few believing friends had given up on him during his "evil" period? Had they said "If this is Christianity, get out of here!" then a great prophet for human dignity would have been lost to the world. Newton's priestly passion still lives on as people everywhere sing "Amazing Grace."

A BIT OF HEAVEN *NOW*

Whenever I am tempted to judge believers who seem narrow-minded, I recall Newton's story. Sometimes we are called to walk with someone very different from ourselves, even with hypocrites (whether liberals or conservatives, atheists or fundamentalists, Buddhists or Muslims, Hindus or Christians). If we believe we can learn something from them, they may want to learn something from us.

> I cannot explain how, but by recounting examples of others' risk-taking faith, mysteriously you may be caught by an Aha! in your own leap of faith.

There's that word *believe* again. But notice it has to do with believing God is speaking through life; it is not belief in a doctrine about God. The God we have come to know (rather than merely think about) is in the matrix of human interactions, in the doubting and believing, the worldly struggles and holy dreams.

Minihistories like these create perspective to inspire ordinary folks to live with passion. Living a bit of heaven *now* is the best way to glimpse heaven *then*.

Reflection Exercise 39. Listening to Springsteen's *The Rising*

Listen to Bruce Springsteen's *The Rising* (www.brucespring steen.net). Pay special attention to the words of "Mary's Place" and "The Rising." How does this seem, or not seem, like prayer? or a psalm of lament? a statement of hope?

Reflection Exercise 40. Your Own Portable Monastery

After working for some time on the phone or at the computer or other project, push your chair back a few inches, with your lap and hands empty. Take a few deep breaths . . . let a line of a poem, scripture, or sacred word come to mind (see Reflection Exercise 10 in Chapter Five). You have entered your portable monastery. After a minute or so, pull your chair back to your work area . . . and continue working. Option: Place an icon, a gong or bell at your workspace; push back to meditate on the icon, or the sound of the gong or bell. (A group example: Try this exercise during a committee or group meeting.)

22

CHOCOLÁT AND SPIDER-MAN

Passionate Gratitude

Surprise is the key to gratefulness. . . . We can learn to let our
sense of surprise be triggered not only by the extraordinary,
but, above all, by a fresh look at the ordinary.
—DAVID STEINDL-RAST, GRATEFULNESS: THE HEART OF PRAYER

Follow your bliss.
—JOSEPH CAMPBELL

If you ask me what I have come into the world to do, I will
tell you: I have come to live out loud.
—EMILE ZOLA

During the oil "scare" in the 1970s, President Jimmy
Carter took to the air to ask the American people for
austerity—lower speed limits, travel less. What if Carter
had done the opposite and asked people to enjoy life more?
Savor a sunset, enjoy a local park, do fun things with family. Too
many people have lost their capacity for enjoyment and wonder.
So suggested Anthony de Mello, a Zen-minded Jesuit priest
from India, in *Awareness: The Perils and Opportunities of Reality*.
Maybe, can we get scared again and still do it?

In malls, airports, and churches, I see faces like the ads I told of earlier—eyes without light, faces without life. At times, my own face reflects the pain of living when passion dries up. Then I notice how someone I care about has gone silent, or my latest dream has fizzled out. Then I think God has withdrawn. But wait—when I get so self-absorbed, I need to lighten up and see a good movie! Come along and watch as passion deepens to compassion, and perspective explodes into extravagant gratitude unleashed into the universe.

CHOCOLÁT AND BABETTE: WILD GRATITUDE

In the movie *Chocolát,* a new store owner causes a sensation in a tiny French village when she opens a little chocolate shop and lavishly begins selling the sweet stuff, giving it away and exuberantly celebrating life. Spouses are thrown off balance when a dried-up partner suddenly comes alive and wants to have sex. Families are thrown into chaos because formerly withdrawn people begin expressing feelings to one another. Worse yet, this all takes place in the penitent season of Lent!

Things reach a crisis. The serene village is now a battleground between the uptight mayor and the free-spirited shopkeeper. She is just having too much fun doing good.

Can you hear the Buddha laughing in the background? Translate just a bit, and watch Jesus tweaking the do-religion-right Pharisee as a woman off the street crashes his party and anoints Jesus' feet with the priciest perfume known to humans.

A wall in my office is covered with icons and pictures from many cultures; one is titled "Jesus Laughing." For Abraham and Sarah, the very idea of having a son in their old age had seemed so silly that they named him Isaac, which means "laughter."

In the Middle East, Africa, and South Asia, you see women working hard all day in gorgeous clothes. In Guatemala one evening about six o'clock, I was on my way back to Panajachel

"Humor is a prelude to faith, and laughter is the beginning of prayer," observed theologian Reinhold Niebuhr. Quaker Elton Trueblood wrote *The Humor of Christ*, pointing out Jesus' frequent riddles, jokes, and wordplays.

from *La Mariposa*, the Butterfly Sanctuary. Suddenly women appeared out of a forest carrying cords of wood on their heads—dressed fit for an inaugural ball. As I walked and talked with a young man in my poor Spanish, one woman's wood began falling piece by piece. Finally, when the last sticks fell, she just stood back and laughed!

Downtown the next morning, empty soda bottles fell off a guy's cart in front of our Jeep. Ahuh! Ahuh! Ahuh! he chortled. From down the street came more laughter.

When I returned home, I said to those around me, "When things go wrong, the first thing let's do is laugh—unless it's a human crisis." Often traveling alone, I now look for ways to laugh aloud to myself and God. One night, as I was catching a quick drink of water and just ready to give a lecture, a naughty faucet sprayed my entire shirt! I laughed a prayer of thanks for a cool shower.

"If in your lifetime the only prayer you offer is 'thank you,' that will suffice," said Meister Eckhart in the fifteenth century. It is hard to express gratitude with a straight face.

> Car radio announces news of war:
> I glimpse my troubled face in rearview mirror.
> Shifting my eyes to sunset I see my countenance lift.

Extravagant gratitude and joyous sacrifice come alive in Isak Dinesen's story (made into a film) *Babette's Feast*. When a French refugee arrives in a little Norwegian town, she is given respite as a servant by two strict elderly sisters whose late father had been the town's pastor. Surprise! After twelve years, Babette gets news she won the lottery. She goes to Paris and spends the entire ten thousand francs.

Babette now returns to throw an extravagant feast for all the disgruntled church and town folk. Present is General Lorenz Lowenheilm, one sister's shy suitor of years ago and now a member of the royal court. At the table, amid frowns and puzzled looks, the general rises to clink his glass. He delivers an address on grace, the grace of God that transcends time and distance, and toasts "a general amnesty" to all. One wild gesture has transformed a community.

Every time I begin a new journal, I copy Dag Hammarskjöld's New Year's poem in *Markings* onto the front page. The first line offers thanks *for* the Presence in the universe, with me in good times and bad; the second offers a toast *to* the One who inhabits the future:

> For all that has been—Thanks.
> To all that shall be—Yes!

SPIDER-MAN: CRAZY COMPASSION

When a mutant spider escapes its tank in a science center to strike an irreversible wound on Peter Parker's hand, all the words in the long-running Marvel comic book series become flesh on the big screen. Which makes us feel more pathos: Peter's hugely swollen hand? His irrepressible urge to zap to the scene and rescue a person in crisis—even an enemy? The weblike gook flowing from his fingers as he dangles limp from a skyscraper? Or is it Spidey's inevitable breakup with his cute lover girl next door, when he must finally kiss off and tell her his crazy double life demands celibate-like compassion? It seems the Way has chosen him. Or, maybe, could he have chosen to die?

If there can be any kind of Christ figure common to all religions, this has to be a major nominee. (His creator is Jewish.)

Spider-Man is pathetic and playful, laughable and honorable, humorous and serious. Peter starts out searching for love but ends up smitten by Love with a capital L. As Spider-Man he is lonely, yet everybody's friend in real life. But what is real? Like the Chocolate Lady and Babette, here you see the holy fool writ larger than life.

FROM FANTASY TO LIVED LIFE

"OK," you say. "That's just the problem. This is all fantasy. It's not practical. Spidey is literally 'off the wall.'" So now I must tell you two stories that I hope will paint a vision to jumpstart the adrenaline of your own gratitude and compassion.

When Professor James Loder taught my wife and me at Princeton, he was likely the headiest thinker I knew. Dry but deep. I would leave with my head abuzz knowing I had been in the presence of genius, but not quite sure how to connect it with life. Then a single incident changed Jim Loder's life forever, as he tells in *The Transforming Moment.*

One day in the 1970s, Jim and his wife were driving along when suddenly they saw a woman in distress by a parked car. They stopped. As Jim attempted to change a tire, the car fell and pinned him beneath it. With a mythical surge of adrenaline, Arlene, Jim's wife, hoisted the car, freeing her injured husband and saving his life. Together, each had become an *avatar*—an incarnation of God, the Christ to a stranger.

Loder had *experienced* Heidegger's *dasein* ("being there"), the Buddha's "present moment," Kierkegaard's "leap of faith," Martin Buber's I-Thou, and the central mystery of sacrifice at the navel of the universe: dying to self so that another might live. After that transforming moment, stu-

> Good myths and fairy tales and art and drama take you to the edges of life—stretch your imagination—and when it is stretched, then little pieces of the impossible suddenly start actually happening.

dents reported how all the intellectual concepts he taught and wrote about came to life, intellect *and* affect, epistemology *and* experience. When he died in 2001, his legacy was not only for brilliant ideas but the brilliance of love.

The second story centers on an ordinary person who paid attention. At midnight on October 13, 1986, a surgeon was telling me that my wife had sustained three lethal injuries, any one of which might take her life by morning. I was not thinking about our car, which was totaled in a head-on crash that morning, nor my broken hand, nor my children's milder injuries. I was not thinking, period. Then I felt a hand on my shoulder. It was Gene, a member of the congregation I served, but not someone I ever had lunch with or saw outside of church. "How did you get here?" I queried. "Well, I took a run before supper, then told my wife something didn't seem right at the Groffs' house" (though our being away overnight was not unusual). "After another walk before bedtime I began calling hospitals in the Harrisburg-Hershey area. And here I am." His presence was surely that of an angel, an *avatar,* a *bodhisattva.* It was also a time of vocational upheaval for me. Gene's hand was the hand of God for me, his face the face of the Christ.

But we are not the Chocolate Lady or Babette or Spidey—or Jim or Gene. We try to extend compassion and get kicked in the teeth. Nikos Kazantzakis's book-turned-film *Zorba the Greek* nurtured many of us and kept us sane through the Kennedy and King assassinations and what would be the lost Vietnam war. We set out to have it all: to love life and save the world, like Zorba. He convinces a young intellectual, Basil, to spend his inheritance on Zorba's ingenious design to restore a Cretan coalminers' town. But by the end, his elaborate dream has crashed. Standing in the rubble, Basil asks Zorba to dance with him, and then the conversation goes like this: "Life is trouble," Zorba continued. "Death, no. To live—do you know what that means? To undo your belt and look for trouble! . . . The highest point a person can attain is not Knowledge, or Virtue, or

Goodness, or Victory, but something even greater, more heroic and more despairing: Sacred Awe!"

Somewhere I learned that "thinking" and "thanking" are related. You begin to think about things and you start to thank; and when you start to thank, you start to feel passionate and compassionate. Awesome!

Reflection Exercise 41. Practicing Daily Gratitude

Record in your journal *Thanks!* for one simple thing each day. (I title mine *¡Gracias!*) Usually this works best in the morning or evening. An option: "art" your thanks using pastels, or create a poem, or note a piece of music that voices your gratitude.

Reflection Exercise 42. Open-Eyed Blessing

This table grace can be used at home or at a community gathering. The leader says: "Be aware of our unity with all people and creation . . . breathing in the same air with rich and poor. . . . Notice the food . . . smells . . . colors. . . . Imagine the seeds . . . the dark soil, the bright sun . . . farmers planting it . . . migrant farm laborers harvesting with their hands. Gently lift your hands on their behalf. Conclude saying the word *¡Gracias!*, meaning both thanks, and grace for those in need, three times in unison: *¡Gracias! ¡Gracias! ¡Gracias!*"

23

LISTEN TO LOVE, TO LOVE

Contemplate Truth, Act Truthfully

The day of my spiritual awakening was the day I saw and
knew I saw God in all things and all things in God.
—Mechtild of Magdeburg, thirteenth-century Beguine mystic

It is necessary to take particular care to begin, if only for a
moment, your exterior actions with this interior gaze and
that you do the same while you are doing them and when
you have finished them.
—Brother Lawrence, The Practice of the Presence of God

Can you recite the whole Torah while standing on one
leg?" Rabbi Hillel was once asked. "Do not do unto
others what you would not want done unto you. This is
the whole Torah," Hillel replied. Confucius said virtually the
same thing. If there is one universal spiritual theme it is this
Golden Rule. Jesus turned the phrase: "Whatever you want others to do to you, do also to them."

CONTEMPLATION: GETTING INSIDE ANOTHER'S SKIN

Somehow it occurred to me that the Golden Rule is not a simple one-dimension humanist plea to do good. Rather, it starts with contemplating the act of another in relation to myself, thus getting outside my own skin. It involves John Keats's idea of negative capability, a momentary capacity to let go of my certainty to get inside another's skin. In the heat of considering an action, this minicontemplation slows me down. Wait a minute: not just what would *I* want—but what would I want done to me if I were in *their* shoes?

Every good action arises out of contemplation. As the mighty Mississippi originates in the still waters of Lake Itasca in northern Minnesota, as Mozart would contemplate a symphony full-blown and then furiously pen the notes on the score, as Barry Bonds contemplates the bat hitting the ball and swings, so action and contemplation form two movements of a seamless whole. "Listen to Love, to love": I am called to contemplate truth and act truthfully. Contemplation is the source of the good act.

But it is not to contemplate abstract truth for my own little self, but truth in relation to another; that is the call of the Golden Rule. Mere thinking cannot love like this, nor mere gritting of my ethical teeth.

Susan Gibson, a bio-tech marketing consultant and Harvard M.B.A. since the late 1980s, tells how hard this is: "There's a lot of pressure *not* to do the right thing," Gibson added, "because the company's livelihood is at risk. I was once asked to market a product that didn't have FDA approval. You don't do it. You need to be OK in your own skin."

> Here's a key difference in postmodern versus primodern views: truth is not relative (anything goes), but relational (what is best for all). This is incarnation: truth gets in your own skin because you got inside someone else's.

Doing the right thing can hurt. Gibson was no longer "viewed as being a team player," she said. "I wasn't trusted to carry the company line." Being OK in your own skin is what this is all about. Get in touch with truth, and then live it.

CONTEMPLATE TRUTH: LISTEN

In Nathaniel Hawthorne's story of *The Great Stone Face,* a boy named Ernest grows up seeing a Great Stone Face in the natural outcropping of a cliff near his home. Over and over, he hears the Native American legend: one day a child will be born in the valley who will grow up and finally bear the exact likeness of the Great Stone Face. All his life he cherishes the story and meditates on that face.

He is disappointed when he does not see the face in a rich man, a famous soldier, a politician, or even a poet whose words echo qualities of the great face. As an older man, Ernest introduces this poet to the people of his village. The poet announces that the Great Stone Face is *Ernest!* He has become what he spent his life contemplating.

"Perhaps the truth depends on a walk around the lake," wrote poet Wallace Stevens. To contemplate truth rather than sequester it could save us from violent certitude. Hawthorne's story of the Great Stone Face points to the Jewish tradition of the imitation of the Holy, and the Christian "imitation of Christ": becoming conformed to the pattern of Love. The great face can take the form of spiritual mentors (Chapter Twenty-Four).

ACT TRUTHFULLY: LOVE

Recently I debated whether to work on a local Habitat for Humanity house. Part of me knew I needed to spend the day writing, but another part knew how physical work would actually be care for my soul. The service project won, and I found

> Contemplation by simple mindfulness in everyday things can be the first ring of the onion, into contemplation of the Holy at the center of all things.

myself still "writing" while pounding nails. For as we volunteer carpenters come and go, each leaving our less-than-perfect windowsills and doorjambs, it creates a funny sort of therapy. (A perfectionist would quit the job before the first coffee break!) It is worth several visits to my psychiatrist to realize that constructing genuine community means building on each other's imperfect beginnings. I need vulnerable community to discern how to love.

How do you discern what is good and true? Religious people are concerned about morality, and so am I. But right listening, not printed rules, is the source of right behavior. "Listen to Love, to love": listen to how deeply you are loved in order to love. If we try to love without contemplating Love, we will give stones for bread.

"Mind your head and watch your step," the flight attendant said as our tiny aircraft taxied into Telluride's mountain airport. There it is: mindfulness guides our steps into the world of moral choices. Listen to Love to discern the most loving choices.

Listening contemplatively, you hear the cries of the world as the call of sacred Love: the interior gaze illumines the exterior act. It is what I call "discernment ethics." This adaptation of the "Wesleyan Quadrilateral" (Methodist in origin) brings us back to a spiritual and moral compass with its four quadrants to discern our way in today's shifting ethical terrain.

A dynamic balance of sacred readings, rational thinking, real experience, and relationships in community (past and present) leads to good choices. Philosopher Charles Hartshorne says this profoundly yet simply: "If we know what experience is, at its best or most beautiful, then and only then can we know

The Wesleyan Quadrilateral

Sacred Text
(reading)

Tradition   **Reason**
(community)   (reflection)

Experience
(action)

how it is right to act; for the value of action is in what it contributes to experiences." The text gets into the texture of your heart in the context of community—and you discover a reason for living that reason knows nothing about.

We do not always make the best choices, but we can listen again to the Lord of Love, who weaves our destiny out of the threads of the choices we make.

Reflection Exercise 43. Contemplative Spin on the Golden Rule

Be attentive for occasions during this week when you feel a quick impulse to react to someone's comment or idea, and then *pause.* Take a deep breath. Imagine for an instant being in that person's skin, inhabiting his or her thoughts. See if the pause affects your response.

Reflection Exercise 44. Contemplating an Act of Goodness

In the Hebrew Psalm 77, the first ten verses are full of confusion and darkness: "My soul refuses to be comforted . . . I am so troubled I cannot speak." Verses 11–12 invite one to meditate on good deeds in the past:

I will call to mind the deeds of the Lord;
I will remember your wonders of old.
I will meditate on all your work,
and muse on your mighty deeds.

Allow some act of goodness to come to mind, where you were
the recipient, the bearer, or the witness to it in another. Meditate on its qualities, surrounding events, its effect on the recipi-
ent(s), and the feelings it creates in you as you meditate. Now
meditate on an opposite situation, one where a person was
demeaned. Notice your feelings. Reflect on the contrasting
qualities, using your journal. In some upcoming decision, be
attentive to those qualities.

24
SINGLING IN COMMUNITY

If your eye is single, your whole body will be full of light.
—JESUS

One does not pray in order to be religious, but to be true to
the grain in one's own wood.
—HOWARD THURMAN

One of the scariest things about losing your religion is feeling so alone. And the scariest thing about returning is fear of getting sucked into unhealthy community. How can you find healthy community that affirms rather than squelches your uniqueness?

SINGLING: ALONE *AND* ALL ONE

One night I was driving by a lake when one of our daughters, age three, asked, "Why is the moon always following us?" Applauding her wonderful question, I recall saying even if there were a thousand cars and a million people on the shore, each would see the moonbeam aimed directly at his or her own feet. Something in the mystery of light makes it so. The more I meditate on the Great Light, the more my unique path is illuminated.

I use *singling* as a verb to express the need of every person to become a distinct self in community, with a unique purpose. "Original blessing" means you are an original work of art, created in "God's own image, male and female . . . and God blessed them." Yet each work of art is created from the clay and dust of all creation. As God is One and Oneness, so is each solitary human being living in solidarity with all. We all breathe.

> Personal spirituality needs the messy membrane of community to be complete.

Sin is a condition in which our original self gets defaced by others' hurts, or from our attempts to please others. This is the source of our ugly actings out—individual *sins* that over time create a false identity. Salvation involves shedding a fake self to get in touch with our true self, restoring our original work of art—like Michelangelo's restored ceiling in the Sistine Chapel. Freedom *from* sin means freedom *for* life.

This is what spiritual practices are for. This is why Howard Thurman said, "One does not pray in order to be religious, but to be true to the grain in one's own wood." It is "the singling of the eye," an ancient phrase meaning that one's heart is undivided. But always it is with an eye toward community. Genuine solitude creates communion.

The more we are *alone,* the more we begin to realize this mystery that we are *all one.* We all breathe. We cannot survive this human brokenness for long without like-minded soul friends. By itself, a child will die; its muscles atrophy without relationships, touching, holding.

> For healthy couples, each partner needs to engage in healthy singleness.

Without the discipline of community, solitude degenerates into isolation and self-absorption; without the discipline of solitude, community degenerates into enmeshment and codependency.

BEING SINGLE IN A COUPLED WORLD

Have you ever been "singled out" in front of others, made to feel different? That feeling describes the desperate cry of many single adults—often painfully orphaned in religious settings—who long to find new forms of faith and family. (I suggest ten such forms in this chapter.) We need new ways to relate to singles today as beacons of light in community, like so many active mystics of the past. Besides, many who are coupled (like me) spend big chunks of time alone. We need creative ways to connect our being alone with being all one.

Spiritual orphans feel rootless and restless, yet one must be exiled from home to find home. In the poem below, I refer to the Hebrew unpronounceable Name *YHWH* ("I Am Who I Am") as I meditate on Cain, who killed his brother Abel and then was given a "mark" for protection. We still kill our own able brothers and sisters, violently or subtly.

YaHWeH
O Name Supreme
who shared our pain
that we might gain
the mark of Cain
and in our exile
all this while
might see your smile
etched in each face
from every race
and know your grace:
I am who I am.
—Genesis 4

Like Cain, we are all marked with a trace of grace. With fellow exiles we stumble home to claim our true identity: I am who I am. Like Cain, we often ignore another's pain and ask, "Am I my brother's keeper?" The answer comes, No, more than that; you are their brother and sister. We are a spiritual community.

MINIMALIST PRACTICES FOR BALANCING SOLITUDE AND COMMUNITY

A twelve-year-old desecrated a nearby synagogue. Police escorted the boy, trembling, with his mother, to see the rabbi. Here is the end of the conversation:

Rabbi: Who are you?
Boy: Jimmy Jones.
Rabbi: Who is Jimmy Jones?
Boy: Uh, I don't know (looking at mother), who am I?
Rabbi: You need to go and find out who you are. Then come back and see me.

Here is the discipline of discovering self in community. Ascetic practices are not meant to spank our fingers, but to help us remember *who* and *where* we are in a world that tempts us to forget in a host of nonplaces—superstores, airports, shopping malls, and Internet sites. Here are ten practices to tend the healthy balance of inner and outer life, self-nurture and self-giving. Without this vital rhythm, we can lose our identity, sell our souls.

When a student went to Cuba, he and his lover each made a pact to keep a journal. His outward journey sparked their unique inward journeys.

FIVE-STORIED SOLITUDE: ALONE

The goal of a daily set-aside meditation time (in Hebrew, *keva*) is to develop a meditative attitude throughout the day (*kavanah*). Pray always, and pray all ways. "Pause and pray" often during the day, to "listen to Love, to love" in your activities.

Here are five practical forms of self-care to quiet our overactive souls and befriend our cocoonlike transformations. Psalms in the Bible (or Bruce Springsteen's contemporary psalms on his album *The Rising*) baptize all the moods of the soul, from anger to despair to bliss. Incorporate physical movement, breathing, poetry, music, silence, dance, and nature in your quiet time. Aim for a minimum of half an hour of personal solitude daily—or at least on four days out of seven.

PRACTICE A SIMPLE "EXAMEN" EACH DAY

At the beginning of each day, notice *gifts* (where have you experienced being loved or loving?), *struggles* (where has it been difficult to love or allow yourself to be loved?), and *invitation* (what is it I need to claim, to become more whole?). If a word or phrase, an image or metaphor comes to mind, begin to repeat it in rhythm to your breathing, or visualize it. . . .

KEEP A SPIRITUAL JOURNAL

Use a journal to reflect on readings, dreams, conversations, quotations, and daily life. (See "Helpful Hints for Keeping a Journal" in the Orientation.)

PRACTICE PHYSICAL AND SPIRITUAL EXERCISES

Try using physical and spiritual exercises to honor your body's need for rest and exercise. Sit and tend to your breathing. Walk or jog. Tai chi or yogalike exercises can open the soul and body. Kneeling or bowing the head scripts a bloated soul to value humility; stretching both hands toward the stars scripts an impoverished soul to claim one's dignity. Find a way every day to kneel and to dance (Reflection Exercise 12).

MEDITATE WITH SACRED TEXTS AND READINGS

The Benedictine fourfold method of *lectio divina* ("divine reading") can be used for sacred texts or any readings: read, reflect, respond, and rest. It can also be practiced with conversations, nature, all of life (see Resource Two).

CULTIVATE SILENCE

Aim for fifteen to twenty minutes of silence to empty the self of clutter, using a centering word or image (Reflection Exercise 10). Promise yourself at least two minutes of silence each morning, no matter how busy you are, even if your regular alone time is later. Take an overnight retreat a couple of times a year in a nearby monastery. An option: Go with a friend, keep the silence, and talk about it on the way back. At home or work, claim bits of retreat in your "portable monastery" (Reflection Exercise 40).

■ ■ ■

The aim of such habits of the heart is to keep your eye on your acorn purpose, a mission for your being on this earth. (See "Life Mission" in Chapter Twenty-Five.)

FIVE-STORIED COMMUNITY: ALL ONE

As Twelve Step groups and Latin American base communities demonstrate, spiritual community can take a variety of forms. Ideally, I aim to have five levels, or "stories," of community in place for myself, so that if one level isn't operative I am not left alone.

RECLAIMING MENTORS, BEFRIENDING STORIES

Recall mentors in your life, and nurture your own and others' stories (Reflection Exercise 45). Notice how your life is already held in a web of community. Extend hospitality to yourself.

FAMILY AND CLOSE FRIENDS

Rekindle relationships with loved ones and friends, whether near or at a distance. As in every tier of community, some are difficult. Yearn to discover lost family members, make new friends, and extend gestures of reconciliation (Reflection Exercise 46). Practice the Serenity Prayer: "God, grant me the serenity to accept the things I cannot change, courage to change the things I can, and the wisdom to know the difference."

SPIRITUAL FRIENDSHIP—FORMAL, INFORMAL

"Spiritual companioning" is a good way to begin this journey again. The Irish call this "soul friends"—*anam cara*. It is as old as David and Jonathan or Ruth and Naomi in Hebrew scripture, or Jesus and the Beloved Disciple in the Gospels, or Rumi and Shams in Sufi tradition. It can be as formalized as a spiritual guide (director) and companion in Christian practice—or the Hesed and Rebbe (seeker and teacher) tradition in Judaism. (Contact Spiritual Directors International at www.sdiworld.org for more information.)

A SMALL COLLEAGUE GROUP

Either find or found a spiritual support group for yourself. I have proclaimed this to myself many times in new communities. Use a book like this one as a catalyst for a small, vital, vulnerable community; watch films, read poetry or fiction together. Include times for silence and reflection, and rituals of closure. How? Start with a bag lunch with a friend, and then each person invites another (see Resource One).

A LARGER FAITH COMMUNITY

People complain about religious community: "That place is dead!" So I choose to speak of "nurturing" community or "life-giving" community. None is perfect, but in a moment I will offer some clues.

■ ■ ■

This is not a left-brain manual on how to "do" church, or mosque, or temple. Rather it is about "being church" or "being temple" for another. If we live with our spiritual eyes open, we never know if another person will reveal the tip of a submerged iceberg, if you or I seem like a "safe person." Then you have found the seed of community.

CLUES FOR LIFE-GIVING COMMUNITY: INTEREST

Out of the rubble of codependency or isolation, how can we find or create some form of life-giving community? I propose two metaphors: *interest* and *bread*.

From the world of finance, I learned "interest follows investment." This is profoundly true in relationships; when I ask someone a simple question and reveal a bit of me, I am investing myself. *Interest* (Latin *interesse*) means "inter-being."

What if we just begin taking more interest in each other? As my children started encountering challenging social situations, I told them what works for me: introduce yourself to another person who's alone, ask a question, and listen with interest.

People are literally dying of loneliness. We can do something now to name this demon that makes orphans out of bright, beautiful people, in lonely office parties, community events, or congregations. If you lead a group, manage a team at work, chair a committee, or conduct worship, coach folks to look for the isolated person in a social gathering; leave the ninety-nine to find the one. Do business talk elsewhere. Treat the newcomer as if she were dying tomorrow and may need a word with you today.

McDonald's big deal is location, location, and location. But spiritually the big deal is connections, connections, and connections. Malcolm Gladwell advocates this in *The Tipping Point*: connections and timing can transform a chance encounter into a genuine relationship or a big cause. Connect with mentors, family, friends, and groups, and trust that you will be led to a life-giving form of larger spiritual community. You are not alone.

After reading this manuscript, one young adult e-mailed me: "I trust God will use your book to speak to me and other spiritual orphans who have no comfortable spiritual home or roots. I pray, in my own way, that we can all see with our eyes, and hear with our ears, with a new sensitivity that can comprehend the light."

In his next e-mail, he wrote: "I would like to change a word in my previous e-mail, from 'comfortable' to 'nurturing.'" Nurture brings us to "bread"—the second metaphor.

CLUES FOR LIFE-GIVING COMMUNITY: BREAD

Breaking bread signifies something sacred in nearly every spiritual tradition, because even unawares we open vulnerable parts of ourselves and create vital connections. We are starved for companions: *com-pain* in French literally means "with bread." I describe my writing and retreat work as "one beggar showing other beggars where to find bread."

A life-giving faith community is an organism first and an organization second. Being part of a life-giving community is like a healthy foot getting directional signals from the rest of the body. Life-giving communities lift up human brokenness instead of ignoring it, tenderly, like bread and wine to be held and blessed. They connect your bread with hungry people beyond the local walls. They foster friendship and small groups. They become a safe extended family for spiritual orphans separated by the gravity of pain or the geography of place. They hear and heal each other's stories. They connect sacred traditions and scriptures with the buried scripts in each other's hearts. They let you grow your own wings, even if yours are a different color from theirs. They coach you to pray, to get in touch with the churnings and yearnings of your own soul.

In a life-giving community you hear a word that comes as a severe mercy, the fierce courtesy only a good friend or a good dream dares to voice. They teach you how to reconcile with others instead of rejecting them. They help you pray your good-byes. The problem with privatized spirituality is the loneliness of nowhere and no one to offer the gift of the fierce courtesy.

Some choose one community for liturgy and music and another for an interfaith project or meditation group. Some-times you may be on sabbatical between faith communities, though still in communion. If you are not part of such an organism, pray to discover one. Or pray and work to change the one you are in, with love.

All of us doubting believers are starving for three joyous lines: "Welcome home. I love you. Supper's ready."

Reflection Exercise 45. Journaling with Mentors

An option: begin with quiet music. . . . Ponder mentors in your life, living or dead (C. S. Lewis is one of mine). . . . Write their names. Pause; think of a present issue where you desire clarity. Scan your list, and choose a mentor to converse with. Begin by stating the issue in your journal. . . . Converse about it with your mentor (in dialogue fashion). . . .

Reflection Exercise 46. Inventory of Intercultural Friendships

Spend time meditating on your friendships. How many are work-related? long-term? short-term? Notice any that are out-side your own familiar circle of culture, race, age, or gender. Would you name any of them as a "soul friend"? Make a few notes. Now put everything aside. Imagine you and your friends being held in a web of love. Be attentive to nudges toward new or renewed friendships. An idea: put a sticky note in your jour-nal a few pages ahead and jot a reminder to ask yourself, How am I praying for (name or concern)?

Reflection Exercise 47. Share and Prayer with a Child

This one-on-one (adult and child) exercise uses two questions: (1) "What's something good happening in your life now (or in our relationship)?" (2) "What's something that has you a bit anxious (or something you would like to see changed)?" The adult answers too; then silently or aloud each one "prays"—which means telling God what each just told the other. (This can be used at bedtime, or adapted when out to eat.) An option: it can be an enriching ritual for couples, or for a single person with another friend.

Reflection Exercise 48. Silent Couple Prayer

Instead of spoken table grace or prayers, try this Quaker-like ritual of allowing silence (start with one minute). Then you may share what each partner was pondering. It allows space for uniqueness yet creates intimacy in silence, and in the sharing. An option: while (or after) discussing a difficult issue, pause for this kind of silence. See if it changes the tone of the conversation or brings clarity to the issue.

25

DANCING YOUR WAY HOME AGAIN

Sankofa

Life must be lived forwards, but it can only be understood
backwards.
—SØREN KIERKEGAARD

Share his pain! We must be in this place as one village!
—MANDINKA ELDER TO KUNTA KINTE, IN ROOTS: THE SAGA OF AN
AFRICAN AMERICAN FAMILY BY ALEX HALEY

The place God calls you to is the place where your deep
gladness and the world's deep hunger meet.
—FREDERICK BUECHNER, WISHFUL THINKING

*S*ankofa portrays a bird with its feet facing forward and its head looking back, usually with an egg in its mouth. "Go back and fetch it" is a good translation. This primal graphic symbol from West Africa expresses Kierkegaard's idea that life can only be understood backwards. *Sankofa* reminds us to keep an eye on our primal past while moving forward into modernity. It echoes Socrates' truth that "the unexamined life is not worth living."

Sankofa

Picture this primodern bird joyously dancing its way through life, feet forward, eyes backward, sideways, head forward again! Go back and fetch the essence of life. Repeated practices of engagement and reflection create the warp and weft of dynamic rituals for individuals, for institutions. Dance is the ideal metaphor for *Sankofa* and the final answer to the question, How shall we then live? "Dance then, wherever you may be!" Dance with all of life's opposites—the personal and the political, your disciplines and delights.

DANCE WITH RIDDLES AND RITUALS

How is it we can taste a palpable sense of the Presence, but just as quickly it disappears? What if this riddle is part of a dance—the light playing hide and seek?

It helped me to learn that *re-velere* in Latin actually means to "re-veil" or "cover again." So revelations are only glimpses of the Sacred that instantly close up again.

Dull ritual*ism* can stifle the spirit, but genuine rituals can recall healing moments. Even a simple ritual, such as how we greet a friend after a long separation, embodies our deep longing for atonement: being at one with, instead of at odds with, or still staying *with* someone even if we are at odds. Healthy rituals allow a secular person to participate in the sacred "as dancing allows the tongue-tied man a ceremony of love," André Dubus wrote in *A Father's Story*.

Between revelations, when I don't feel particularly spiritual, I am carried by ritual: singing or repeating prayers of others as in *The Book of Common Prayer* (which is still a best-seller). The dance goes on amid the riddles and rituals that keep me longing for the Presence, even in the absence. I try to keep in step as the light plays hide and seek.

DANCE WITH ABILITIES AND DISABILITIES

Recently, all the bad feelings I had in second grade came crashing in on me, while sitting in a seminar at the feet of a mentor I know and love. As page numbers were called out, I was still meditating with the idea just presented. I tried looking on my neighbor's pages—but got hopelessly lost. For me, to share this has taken years of looking back.

Descartes said, "I think, therefore I am." But only in my middle years did I discover dyslexia had been a big part of why I couldn't "think" right—and therefore felt bad about who "I am"—which is radically right-brained. This is why the multiple-intelligences approach to learning has been such a spiritual breakthrough for me.

Consequently I enlist human angels to help me sequence things, while my spontaneous insights keep things lively for others. I quip that one of my favorite "hymns" is the Beatles' line about getting by with "A Little Help from My Friends." Someone quips back, "You know the next line?" I say "Sure, about getting high with a little help—that too!"—because my keen sense of the Presence often fades but gets rejuvenated in community. And getting "high" in pop culture masks a yearning for the Most High.

My short attention span signals to me that if I am getting bored, so is the group. Therefore I weave my presentations into unified short segments—minilectures, conversing in groups, times for music and movement—and periods of silence. It keeps everyone awake.

The ability to find a gift in disability is one of the mystery miracles of this Spirit life. By sharing my learning differences, bipolar struggles, and parenting hassles, others find their own experiences validated by mine. Many tell me they have never heard these things named from a lectern or pulpit, and never as an invitation to mine bits of grace in the grit.

DANCE WITH THE *I* AND THE *WE*

Modern Western culture is geared to the aggressive individualist. Whether trying to take over the Wild West or create a new philosophy, a lot of us guys step on minorities and women. Can't we all learn a new step for this dance? to step *between* instead of *on top of* each other's feet? or walk for a moon in others' moccasins before criticizing their steps?

Descartes's big statement—"I think, therefore I am"—was given to him by an angel in a dream. But oddly, from then on he seemed to favor thinking and leave the dreaming to Jung and Freud. Most moderns still get their identity on the basis of their thinking skills, but one who has learning differences is taught to think less of oneself.

Instead of Descartes's idea of finding your identity in your personal brain, I have come to treasure its African counterpoint: "I am, because we are: and since we are, therefore I am" *(ubuntu ungumuntu ngabantu* in Zulu). "A person is a person because of others." Africans value community before the individual because without community, no individuals could survive.

Nellie lived alone in the house behind us when we were in the Philadelphia area. She used to say: "We are surely pleased to have you. . . . We have lived here for sixty-nine years. . . . We have always found some small way to help out anybody in trouble, and we have never found ourselves wanting."

Who were the *we*? her cat Smoke and herself? a vestige of her parents' language from her large childhood family, now unthinkingly part of her single state of being? some native awareness of her African ancestors? or Nellie and God? Whatever it was, our children still remember her *we* language. Recently I learned that singer Ella Fitzgerald used this *we* language too.

> I am bothered by a failure to speak of justice in much of today's spirituality. It echoes a split life rather than the nonsplit life. Suspect any spirituality that is "just us"—too much *me* and not enough *we.*

In *Roots,* Alex Haley describes his ancestor, Kunta Kinte, down in the death-dealing hold of the slave ship. Another Gambian captive, not of Mandinka language like Kunta, screams unintelligibly as the white "toubob" captors whip him. The clear voice of an elder calls out to Kunta in Mandinka: "Share his pain! We must be in this place as one village!"

Once I asked Haley if that sentence could be the storyline for the readers of *Roots:* "Share the pain with all Kuntas! We must be in this place today as one global village!" "No . . . ," he hesitated, and then boldly proclaimed, "Yes! That *is* what I mean."

Sometimes I cry composite tears alone. Sometimes I laugh on behalf of the cosmos.

> I hope the questions I raise and stories I tell begin to mend the tattered threads of your own half-fulfilled mission into the great fabric of the universe.

Both experiences are part of *tikkun olam*—the kabalistic phrase that means "to repair the universe." Your life mission becomes a microchip in mending the universe.

LIFE MISSION: DANCE BETWEEN FOCUS AND FREEDOM

"The surf that distresses the ordinary swimmer produces in the surf-rider the super-joy of going clean through it." Early YMCA leader Oswald Chambers gives us this image for the inner aptitude to rise to the challenge of stress. It is not ignoring but using the resistance.

A life mission statement is a platform for leaning into life's stress, to create playful projects for serious purposes. The stress that throws the ordinary person off-balance produces in the disciple a superjoy that sees you clean through it.

"The person with a *why* to live can endure almost any *how*"—almost any circumstances. This is how Victor Frankl distilled the wisdom of survivors in death-dealing concentration camps in his classic book *Man's Search for Meaning*. As Jesus expressed it, "If your eye is single, your whole body will be full of light."

Having a single focus for your life creates a healing of purpose. It is your unique expression of "Listen to Love, to love." Your mission statement is your *why* for living, and that is the real reason for engaging in healthy habits of the heart.

In the film *Billy Elliot*, Billy falls as he tries to dance. His teacher tells him to keep his eye on a spot on the wall—and it becomes an eloquent duet between focus and freedom. With focus, our cycling around with all its fallings and risings will spiral into a joyous life mission (see Reflection Exercise 49).

Test your mission. "Follow your bliss," Joseph Campbell said over and over to summarize primal myths. It does not mean "If it feels good, do it." Rather, it is a test to discern a genuine call: *follow* is a disciple word implying obstacles, pilgrimage; *your* means that your path is unique, no one else's; *bliss* will issue in blessing, not destruction.

In the moment of self-forgetting love, you may let go of your prized mission. It is Zen-like wisdom: make a plan, give up a plan.

DANCING WITH FAITH INSIDE OUT

"The Pilgrimage Issue"—so reads the surprising subtitle of a recent *New York Times Magazine* issue, "Fashions of the Times." The last page is titled "Pilgrim's Progress." Though few youthful *Times* readers have likely read John Bunyan's classic *Pilgrim's Progress*, they all write home about their posh pilgrimages to the world's pop shrines.

> Gerard Manley Hopkins said, "Myself it speaks and spells / Crying *What I do is me: for that I came.*" So an authentic life mission embodies the unity of one's being and doing.

We all yearn for a sacred secular pilgrimage worth writing home about. But the spiritual tweak on leisure pilgrims is not lost on us. No matter that the *Times Magazine* issue is about clothing fashions. Since September 11, 2001, Amy M. Spindler writes in her feature article, "the pilgrimage issue" is *the* issue: "Our only certainty is what we do not know. And whether as a result or just a reaction, a curious wanderlust has cast its spell on fashion and the world it dresses. Our search is a kind of spiritualism that defies our former hand-on-hips agnosticism. Both literally and figuratively, we seek the world outside ourselves to look inside."

We seek the world *outside* ourselves to look *inside*. Could this be a statement about primodern faith? Once, it was assumed that faith started inside ourselves; then we took it into the world outside. But for many, today's spiritual journey begins by seeking the world outside ourselves that leads us to discover a new kind of faith inside.

It works either way, and you are still saved by grace. Dag Hammarskjöld, secretary general of the United Nations in the 1960s, wrote in his journal, *Markings,* "In our era, the road to holiness necessarily passes through the world of action."

The traditional sequence of "faith and works" runs this way: "Believe the right things, then do the good thing." Yet the origin of be-*lieve* is intensely personal, from the Old English *leof,* meaning "cherished, loved, or longed for." Add the prefix *be-* and what we cherish affects our being, makes us who we are.

Be Longing

Our grieving creates a belonging
that begets our believing—
until a knowing
inhabits our longing.

We are all born into a world that breaks us through too much success, or too much failure. We are born homesick. This holy longing creates a web of community that gives us courage to risk.

A primodern sequence might look like this: "Immerse yourself in the world of action, and that will draw forth your faith." To adapt an Estonian proverb, "The work will teach you how to do it"—and why you do it.

"I make myself rich by making my wants few." Henry David Thoreau's words convey minimalist essentials for how we need to live and what we need to know. Living simply, with gratitude and compassion, in a complex world teaches us what we need to know spiritually. We can align our path to that compass.

Eventually, at least in death if not in life, we will finally lose our "religion"—even our attachments to what we think is so important. The good news is we do not need to wait for the crisis. We become truly blessed if we learn the art of detachment, letting go of illusion while we are still living.

An Aztec prayer (Resource Five) says: "O for so short a time, we are on loan to each other." *O for so short a time;* live with passionate gratitude. *We are on loan to each other;* work for just compassion.

THE ONLY LIFE WORTH LIVING

If the only thing in this terrific, terrifying world we can know for sure is that we cannot believe in a certain future, then what we need to know for sure is that the mystery of Love will keep rising out of the rubble. This is what we can know from experience deeper than believing anything or any thing.

To pray is to yearn. Everybody, in that sense, is praying; it is simply the word we use to express the primal longing for what we cherish deeply. Believing occurs when we *consciously* affirm that deep longing. Tell me your yearnings, and I will tell you your prayers.

Soon disciples of the Lord of Love may once again be called simply "followers of the Way" as in the Bible's early Acts of the Apostles. For these primal stirrings draw all people who follow the Way of *receiving life, dying to self-deceit,* and *giving back.* And that for me is the trinity of experience, and the only Way worth living.

Reflection Exercise 49. A Life Mission Statement

Enter in your journal: *I am here on this earth to. . . .* Let your mission statement reflect this twofold focus: What puts a sparkle in your eyes? Some deep gladness within you? What pulls at your heartstrings? Some deep hunger of the world? Avoid being too general ("to love everyone") or too specific ("to lay bricks"). Put *your* flesh on *your* mission ("to express love *through* the building blocks of my life, or *by* creating . . ."). Word it in a way that speaks to your working years or your retirement . . . even disability. Rework your mission; keep it short. Repeat it as a prayer of your heart; put it on a card inside your closet or desk or wallet.

Additional resources: Steven Covey's *Seven Habits of Highly Effective People;* Richard Bolles's *What Color Is Your Parachute?;* and Lori Beth Jones's *The Path.*

Reflection Exercise 50. The Clearness Committee

The "clearness committee" (developed by Quakers in relation to marriage) is now adapted for individuals facing a variety of vocational issues. The "focus person," the one seeking clearness, writes up his or her situation in advance and circulates it to five or six trusted persons whom he or she invites, asking one to serve as convener and another as note taker. The convener begins the meeting with silence and then invites a fresh statement of the concern by the focus person. This is followed by silence again, and by discerning questions: "Have you considered . . . ?" (but not fix-it advice of the sort "Why don't you . . . ?"). Use observations as well: "I'm hearing four possible careers." All this is done in a meditative atmosphere—and may end with a spoken or physical blessing, like clasping right hands with the presenter's hands. The group may be reconvened.

An option: A life mission statement, night dreams, or day dreams can be included in notes for a clearness committee.

DEBRIEFING AND HOMEWORK
Chop Wood and Carry Water

In the Orientation I suggested that you frame this entire book as my inviting you into many rooms in a world museum. Think of the stories I told as pictures or artifacts in those rooms. In halls and alcoves you have explored various styles of art and music, vistas of perspective, and commentaries on their meanings. You may have stood and gazed with van Gogh, skipped over the Beatles to ponder Bach, or gotten bored and slipped outdoors to hear Springsteen. As in a museum, if you try to absorb all the pieces equally your brains will be fried. But by pausing with a few, now you leave to see the world differently, to really *see* the beauty and pain of reality—and see Beauty in Reality.

I hope you find yourself listening to those you love with new ears, speaking to those who are unloved in a new voice, and engaging in your work with new vision.

The only work that matters is homework, engaging in the work that brings you home to your true self and the Truth Force at the heart of the universe. It may be work that no one

At a party, after too much beer, an American friend heard himself say he would go back to Ireland. For more than two decades, he and his Irish wife have directed a reconciliation community among Irish youth and their parents.

else values, but it is the treasure of your life if it brings you home. It may be the same work as before you read this book— you chop wood and carry water again. But now, just when you're not looking, one stick of kindling catches fire or one drop of experience becomes a prism. Your compass is within. You stand on tiptoe, while that still sacred moment illumines your universe.

Author's note: I have written for all, Buddhist or Christian, Muslim or Jew, Hindu or apatheist—one who doesn't care about the God-issue, but often cares about people. What follows is a P.S. for sometime followers of Jesus, but I invite any of you to listen in.

P.S. FOR ONCE OR MAYBE CHRISTIANS

How Big Is Your Jesus?

I am recovering the claim that Jesus was not crucified
in a cathedral between two candles, but on a cross
between two thieves; on the town garbage heap; at a
crossroad so cosmopolitan that they had to write his title
in Hebrew and in Latin and in Greek . . . at the kind of
place where cynics talk smut, and thieves curse, and
soldiers gamble. Because that is where he died.
And that is what he died about. And that is where
Christians ought to be, and what Christians should be about.
—GEORGE MACLEOD, FOUNDER OF THE IONA COMMUNITY, SCOTLAND

I will not leave you orphaned; I am coming to you.
In a little while the world will no longer see me,
but you will see me; because I live, you also will live.
—JESUS IN JOHN 14

A friend tells this story about going through customs
inspection on the way back from Haiti. The person
ahead of him had bought lots of costly jewelry but was
waved through by the customs officer with a mere glance. My
friend had only an inexpensive carved head of Jesus. But it was

big, about knee-high, so he had wrapped it in several layers of towels in a burlap bag. As the officer dug deeper into the towels, expecting expensive hidden items, suddenly he looked up and asked, "How big is your Jesus, anyway?"

That is *the* question for third-millennium Christians. I am convinced the more we drink from the unique well of Christ, the more we will connect with the universal underground stream that draws all people of faith.

THE ONLY WAY? (AND MANY ROOMS): JOHN 14:1–6

"I am the way, and the truth, and the life. No one comes to the Father but by me." Extremists misuse this exclusive-sounding text to kill or convert people against their will. But I want to show how this text about the "only way" and "many rooms" in John 14:1–6 is one of the most *inclusive* in the Bible. Jesus may not have said these exact words, but they echo the voice of Jesus through the community back *then*. What do they say to us *now*?

"I am the way. . . . No one comes . . . but by me." But what is the way? And who is the *me* that is the only way? Jesus was very clear about that in Matthew 25: "Just as you did it to one of the least of these who are members of my family, you did it to me." During Jesus' brief ministry he went around touching the lives of people on the edges of society: lepers and tax collectors, filthy rich folks and beaten-down widows, prostitutes and Roman military officials—this despite his clear pacifist teaching.

In high-tech culture, we long to touch Jesus and be touched, like doubting Thomas, who said, "Unless I see the mark of the nails in his hands . . . and put my hand in his side, I will not believe" (John 20:25). The beautiful thing is that by touching the broken lives of "the least of these"—

> A lot of us doubting believing disciples understand why doubting Thomas is called "the Twin," because he's one of us.

people with AIDS, prisoners, dehydrated children and their starving parents—we actually get to touch the living Christ in the wounds of others.

To ignore the least of these is to miss the only way. It is the Way of the cross, the place where brokenness becomes a doorway to blessing. It is as if Jesus says, "Meet me at the edges, in the marginal people and marginal parts of yourself, for that is the only way to see me rise at the center." Jesus enfleshed the primal Way of life-giving sacrifice at the navel of the universe (Hindu *Rig Veda);* "the Lamb that was slain from the creation of the world" (Revelation 13:8, NIV). It is the *Tao Te Ching,* the "Way that has Power"—by whatever name.

All this rings true to the Easter appearances. Jesus seems unconcerned about name recognition: appearing in the guise of a gardener at the tomb, a stranger on the road to Emmaus, an advice-giving fisher on the shore. When two disciples' eyes are opened and they recognize Jesus in the breaking of the bread at Emmaus, he disappears! At the tomb, when Mary recognizes the gardener is Jesus, she is told: "Do not hold on to me!" The final judgment of a true disciple is to be in touch with the least of these in genuine self-forgetting love: "Lord, when did we see you hungry? . . ." That is the Truth.

This is what it means to be called "followers of the Way"—the way that is revealed in the *Acts* of the Apostles— (the *mitzvoth* in Hebrew), the deeds that give life to the Word, and the only way worth living. That is the Life.

MANY ROOMS? (AND THE ONLY WAY): JOHN 14:1–6

Primodern faith wants to hold together the paradox of the only way (John 14:6) with the many rooms (John 14:2): "In my father's house there are many rooms." This is the voice of the same Jesus who says in John 10, "I have other sheep that do not belong to this fold." If ever there was a time when we need to think of various traditions of the Way as rooms in the world's one big house, it is now. In *The Next Christianity,* Philip Jenkins warns of new crusades, in a mix of religious and political enemies. But in *Mere Christianity,* C. S. Lewis gives us the wisest of words about these many rooms: "When you have reached your own room, be kind to those who have chosen different doors and to those who are still in the hall. If they are wrong, they need your prayers all the more, and if they are your enemies, then you are under orders to pray for them. That is one of the rules common to the whole house."

WHAT MIGHT THE CHURCH OF THE WAY LOOK LIKE IN THE THIRD MILLENNIUM?

I leave you with three more story-pictures that can serve as icons of hope for what one solitary life can do in solidarity with fellow pilgrims.

> People were abuzz at the adult class in an inner-city church. Police had arrested a young man for breaking in and stealing a computer from the church office. "Too bad," members complained; it was one more sign of the deteriorating neighborhood. Bud Smith, a soft-spoken retiree, quietly asked had anyone been to the county jail to visit the suspected youth? After an awkward silence, Bud said he would visit the prisoner. The gesture of that single visit began a long-term relationship with the troubled neighborhood youth. Bud gained a new understanding of the inner city youth and their problems and shared his experiences and got church people involved. As neighborhood families noticed the church's changing attitude, new bridges were built between Hope church and its community. The seed was in a question. The power was in a gesture.

I once served a congregation in which lots of women had blue hair. Now some younger folks have blue or purple hair. Why is it they are not just as welcome?

Mike is an ordained priest but calls himself a spiritual orphan, serving as a counselor in a psychiatric center. He quotes a line from *The Book of Common Prayer:* "These eyes of mine have seen the Savior." Mike says, "I would just like to see the Savior."

One day he e-mailed me: "I'm just seeing folks. Saw a 17 year old whose girlfriend is pregnant, saw a 32 year old whose stepson is beating up on her infant, saw a woman who spent time in a federal prison. I guess my day was a far cry from the days where I worried about getting on the right committees!" I merely observed that he did not write, "I *met* with . . ." but "I saw. . . ." Could he be seeing the Savior in the least of these? In his next e-mail note, he said: "You know, I've been looking for Jesus in all of the wrong places! Today I saw an autistic kid who smiled at me. Amazing."

Near San Diego a cross standing on public land became the cause of a big community fight, as an Atheist Coalition got the permit to use it on Easter morning. Jesus would not be so concerned about that as over the hateful ways some of his disciples attacked other human beings. However, one Christian group baked muffins and quietly served them to the atheists as they gathered that Easter dawn. There was the church; there was the gospel.

The Christian mystery says that God has entered the stuff of this world and is present in Christ through the Spirit to transform brokenness into blessing. I see this truth verified wherever inklings of transforming Love occur—in the church or in the world, in nature or in human lives.

It is the truth of experience, as Albert Schweitzer wrote in the concluding paragraph of *The Quest of the Historical Jesus:*

Jesus comes to us as One unknown, without a name, as of old, by the lake-side, to those who knew not. . . . and speaks to us the same word: "Follow me!" . . . And to those who listen, whether wise or simple, this One will be revealed in the toils,

> Learning to respond rather than react to life's surprises, in a way that blesses the world and your own soul: this is what Plato meant by "the education of desire"—that every manner of thing be transformed for good.

the conflicts, and the sufferings which they shall pass through in this company, and, as an astounding mystery, they shall learn in their own experience who this One is.

So we journey alongside the Jesus of history into the Christ of experience, who bears good news for spiritual orphans: "I will not leave you orphaned; I am coming to you. . . .You will see me."

And the Way this Servant Lord comes to us is through the down-and-out and the up-and-out folks on the edges of the world and at the edges of your life. If you follow, the Jesus you see is as big as the Milky Way, infusing particles of Love into our far-flung universe. But if you stay near the still waters, you can look down and see the moonbeam aimed directly at your feet to point you home again.

RESOURCE ONE
GUIDELINES FOR GROUP
GATHERINGS

Ground Rules: Confidentiality. No advice giving, only questions or reflections, stories or observations. Methods of sharing: Option one is conversational exchange as a group. Option two is focused time on each person (five to ten minutes), followed by five minutes for attentive conversation with that person and then transition to the next (time estimates depend on the size of the group). Note: Resources Three and Four below may also be adapted.

Convener: The convener's role is to keep track of ground rules and time according to the group's options. At the end of each meeting, choose a convener for the next time.

Gathering: Convener or another may choose an object to place in the center—a candle, bowl, stone, or other symbol from nature. Convener: open the group with a few minutes of silence. . . . Break the silence with a brief invitation to share (a quotation, prayer, poem, or music).

- Invite any person to share questions or reflections.
- Be comfortable with silence.
- Be attentive to one another.
- Keep the focus on the person sharing.
- Ask open-ended questions or offer observations.

Option one: free-flow conversation

Option two: create a transition to next person (see item 5
under Closure)

Closure: Find a ritual of closure, or one that the leader has suggested. Examples:

1. Join hands and sing a line of a song, such as "Amazing
   Grace."
2. Say the Serenity Prayer (Chapter Twenty-Four), the words
   of the Aztec Prayer (Resource Five), or a relevant quote.
3. Turn left palm up, right palm down, and join hands—a
   symbol of receiving (left) and giving (right), silently.
4. Join right hands in center (like spokes in a wheel or cross
   roads), and then have each person place left hand on shoulder of person on left.
5. Pass around a stone, candle, or other object, silently. (Varia-
   tion: this can be done during sharing as well, using an
   object as a "talking stick," and then passing it to the next
   person, who shares.)
6. Bless the person on your right, in a single sentence blessing
   (or silently), following by speaking "Let it be," the cue for
   the next person. *Amen* (Hebrew, "Let it be so"), often spoken in unison to end a prayer, can sound strange in modern
   ears. So I suggest that groups say "Let it be" as a unison
   affirmation after a spoken prayer or blessing.

RESOURCE TWO
PERSONAL
MEDITATIVE READING

This ancient form of "sacred reading" *(lectio divina)* was originally designed for scripture, but it can be used with various kinds of reading. Benedict in the fifth century used the image of meditating on a text "like a cow chewing her cud." Guigo II in the twelfth century outlined the *Lectio* in four steps, beginning with silence and ending in incarnation:

Silence: "Be still and *know.*"
- *Reading* (Read) grazing—select and read a brief text silently, or aloud.
- *Meditating* (Reflect) chewing—reread it, ponder its context and meanings.
- *Praying* (Respond) ruminating—let it get down in your gut; listen to your life.
- *Contemplating* (Rest) digesting—just be, "lost in wonder, love, and praise."

Incarnation: Embody love; "the word becomes flesh" in your active life.

There are two especially helpful ways of doing the responding praying stage: (1) notice a phrase that lures you—or disturbs you, be with it, and repeat it, or (2) use your imagination, visualize a scene in a story, converse with the characters in your mind, or use a journal.

An option: adapt the *lectio* to life. Use the process to meditate on a line of conversation, a friend's countenance, a feeling in your gut, a shimmering tree, a story, a poem, or a song.

RESOURCE THREE
GROUP
MEDITATIVE READING

The group *lectio divina* (literally, *divine reading*) is a method of reading and sharing a short text in a group of four to seven to connect it to the context of your life. (In a large conference, several such groups can be formed and can meet concurrently in the same room.) Choose a one-to-two-minute portion of a sacred scripture or spiritual reading (maybe from this book), poetry, fiction, or even music. An option: You could watch a clip from a film three times, using this same format.

Begin by choosing a convener, who may read the text or call on others to read, and who moderates the conversation.

Convener: Call the group to a brief time of silence. Then offer a spoken invitation to listen for some word each needs to hear.

First reading: Listen for a word or phrase that shimmers—one that lures you or disturbs you. Allow silence, and then each person shares *only* an image for now, without comment.

Second reading: Allow silence to reflect on an experience or feeling connected to the word phrase, or image. Each person shares a story or feeling with the group, as seems right for you. (Keep it personal: use *I* and *me* rather than *we* and *us*. Minimize crosstalk; receive each other's story as a gift.)

Third reading: Be attentive to some action or response you feel called to this week. Allow silence (or break for a longer silence *and set a time to reconvene*). After the silence, each person shares a response or action. (It may be as simple as a call to meditation on some concern, to call or write someone, or to begin keeping a journal.)

Closure: One by one, each offers the person on his or her right a single sentence of blessing—or they can do it silently followed by speaking "Let it be"—the cue for the next person. (See other methods of closure in Resource One.) For a large gathering, sit quietly till all other groups are silent.

Notes: This method comes out of monastic practice, where it was called *collatio* (root of the word "collating"), originally "the bringing together" of a shared supper. It is a bringing together of friends and stories and the connections they bring, related to a short reading. It is used in meetings, lunch breaks in a work situation, and in "base communities" of third-world countries where Bible study, prayer, singing, personal compassion, and social action often merge. It is a unique way to create small-group depth even in a large gathering or space. (Allow a half hour, longer if you are extending time at the third reading.)

RESOURCE FOUR
FAITH FINDING, FAITH SHARING

For use in a group, class, retreat, at work, home or worship, or over a meal

Leader: Briefly summarize the entire exercise and explain its purpose: to connect faith with daily life. It is faith sharing "from below," so each person stands on an equal footing. Note: this can be used with small groups or large audiences.

Announce: "Choose someone with whom you will share in a few minutes. Just turn to the person next to you, or you can all get up and mix around till everyone is linked with someone." Invite everyone to be seated; create a quiet atmosphere. Then announce:

Step 1. "Think over the past week (or other period of time), and notice a problem you've had to deal with in some area of your life." (Allow a few minutes of silence.)

Step 2. "Contemplate: How has divine Love—or human friendship or prayer, or faith, or a community of faith—made a difference in how you responded to that problem?" (Allow a few minutes of silence.) Then find a simple way to break the silence: a spoken "Let it be," the ringing of a quiet chime, or a sentence of invitation such as "Let us be attentive to each other as we share."

Step 3. "Turn to the person you just met, share the issue or concern, and reflect with your neighbor on how some aspect of faith made a difference." (Announce length of time for sharing—six to ten minutes total, three to five minutes per person.)

Step 4. After sharing, invite each pair to spend one minute in silence. "Try closing your eyes and picturing the face of the one next to you, lifting up that person's needs and gifts." (An option: "Offer a 'sentence of blessing' for each other—but use the discipline of only one sentence!") "When you are ready, give your friend some sign of peace."

Step 5. End as seems natural with the whole group harvesting their insights. Ask, "What did we learn about faith sharing?" Conclude with a song or blessing.

RESOURCE FIVE
"O FOR SO
SHORT A TIME"

O For So Short a Time

Aztec Prayer

Kent Ira Groff, 2004
arr. Mary J. Morreale, 2004

Freely with expression
May be sung as a round

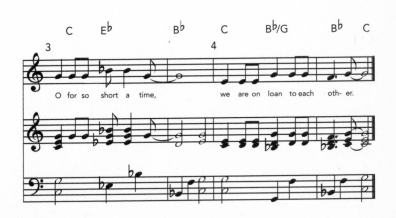

NOTES

ORIENTATION

The verse by Gabriela Mistral is taken from *Burning Bright: An Anthology of Sacred Poetry*, ed. Patricia Hampl (New York: Ballantine, 1995), p. 149.

PART ONE. THE GIFT IN THE GRIT

The quotation from Brother Lawrence of the Resurrection is in *The Practice of the Presence of God,* trans. by John Delaney (Doubleday, 1977), p. 70. The lyrics from Robert Hunter are published on *The Annotated "Scarlet Begonias,"* by arrangement with Ice Nine Publishing Company, San Rafael, Calif. http://arts.ucsc.edu/GDead/AGDL/scarlet.html

1. BEING AGNOSTIC CRACKS THE DOOR TO TRUTH

Alan Jones is quoted in *U.S. Catholic,* Nov. 2001 issue. The epigraph by Arthur Koestler is from *The Sleepwalkers* (New York: Macmillan, 1968), ch. 2. Figures on young believers in Britain are from an interview by Ralph C. Wood, "The World of P. D. James: Deep Mysteries" in *Christian Century,* Sept. 27-Oct. 4, 2000, *117*(26), p. 964. The Barna statistics are reported by Patrick Jansen in "Customizing: Church for the Unchurched" in *NETResults,* July-Aug. 2003, *24*(5), p. 24. The story from the Buddha is adapted from Thich Nhat Hanh, *Being Peace* (Berkeley, Calif.: Parallax Press, 1987), pp. 42–43.

2. BIG BARRIERS TO BELIEVING

The lyrics by Jim Croce are from his album *I'll Have to Say I Love*

You/Salon and Saloon, ABC-11424, USA, 1973. "Those who find their life . . ." is in Mark 8:35. Garrison Keillor's joke is from *Wobegon Boy* (New York: Viking Penguin, 1997), pp. 135–136. On "a single eye," in rabbinic tradition there is an expression "the singling of the eye"; in Eastern thought, "the third eye"; in the American deist period, "meditation's eye." In Matthew's Gospel, Jesus says, "If thine eye be single, the whole body will be full of light" (Matthew 6:22, King James Version) and speaks to Mary: "One thing is necessary" (Luke 10:39). For Søren Kierkegaard, "purity of heart" means "to will one thing." It is what *The Book of Common Prayer* means by serving with "gladness and singleness of heart." Lauren Winner's remark is in "A Return to Tradition? Gen X Revisited," *Christian Century,* Nov. 2–8, 2000, *117*(31), p. 1146. The quote from Rebbe Nachman of Breslov is in David A. Cooper, *Silence, Simplicity, and Solitude* (New York: Bell Tower, 1992), p. 81. I am indebted to Nancy Brubaker, Lancaster, Pa., for the idea of "losing track of time."

3. HIDE AND SEEK IN STUFF

Pierre Teilhard de Chardin's epigraph is from *The Divine Milieu* (New York: Harper & Row Perennial Library, 1968), p. 66. The one by Arlene Helderman is in the chapter "Spiritual Orphan" in *God Within: Our Spiritual Future—As Told by Today's New Adults,* ed. Jon M. Sweeney (Woodstock, Vt.: Skylight Paths, 2001), p. 56. "The Word became flesh . . ." is in the Gospel of John 1:14 (author's translation in text); on God having "hidden these things," see Luke 10:21 and Matthew 11:25; on "God chose what is foolish . . ." see Paul's letter 1 Corinthians 1:18, 27. K. M. George writes about the Russian holy fools in *The Silent Roots: Orthodox Perspectives on Christian Spirituality* (Geneva: World Council of Churches Publications, 1997), p. 58. Jung wrote, in *Modern Man in Search of a Soul,* trans. W. S. Dell and Cary F. Baynes (New York: Harvest/Harcourt Brace Jovanovich, 1933), that by age thirty-five, every crisis was basically a religious one (p. 229).

4. THE "VULGAR" BIBLE

The epigraph and quote about "defilement" is from Simone Weil, *Gravity and Grace,* trans. Arthur Mills (Lincoln, Ne.: University of Nebraska Press, 1992; originally published by Putnam's, 1952). The text of the *Shema* begins, "Hear, O Israel: The Lord your God, the

Lord [is] one; and you shall love . . ." (Deuteronomy 6:4, NIV). The Dietrich Bonhoeffer quote is from *Life Together* (New York: Harper, 1954), p. 97. The story and quote about Herbert's poem is from Simone Weil, *Waiting for God,* trans. Emma Crauford (New York, Harper, 1973), pp. 68–69. Evelyn Underhill's comment is from *The Spiritual Life* (Harrisburg, Pa.: Morehouse, 1999) p. 55.

5. YEARNING YOUR WAY HOME

The Novalis quotation is from John Berger, "You Can't Go Home: The Hidden Pain of 20th Century Life," *Utne Reader* (May–June, 1990), pp. 85–87. The Andy Warhol epigraph is by Holland Cotter, "Everything About Warhol But the Sex," *New York Times,* July 14, 2002. Somerset Maugham, *Of Human Bondage* (New York: Doubleday, 1936), p. 106, continues: "But the young know they are wretched, . . . full of the truthless ideals which have been instilled into them, and each time they come in contact with the real they are bruised and wounded." Daniel Levinson and coauthors write in *The Seasons of a Man's Life* (New York: Knopf, 1978) that no man can get to age forty without some experience of human destructiveness; Gail Sheehy, in *Passages* (New York: Bantam, 1977), says much the same for men and women. Recall also the comment by Jung at the end of the note for Chapter Three. Pascal is quoted in Diogenes Allen, *Three Outsiders: Pascal, Kierkegaard, and Simone Weil* (Cambridge, Mass.: Cowley, 1983), p. 31. See also *Mind on Fire: A Faith for the Skeptical and Indifferent from the Works of Blaise Pascal,* ed. James M. Houston (Minneapolis: Bethany House, 1997), p. 88, Fragment 121–418). On *via positiva* and *via negativa,* Pseudo-Dionysius, in the late fifth century, speaks in his Mystical Theology God's presence as a dark ray. His work is a masterful weaving of Eastern and Western ideas. The poetry of Ecclesiastes 3:1–11 illustrates this rhythm of "embracing and refraining from embracing." On John and Jesus, see Luke 7:33–35 and 7:18–23. "I believe, help my unbelief": see Mark 9:24. "They worshipped him, but some doubted": see Matthew 28:17. The quote from Thomas Merton is in *Faith and Violence: Christian Teaching and Christian Practice* (Notre Dame, Ind.: University of Notre Dame Press, 1994), p. 213. The quote from Frederick Buechner is in *Wishful Thinking: A Theological ABC* (New York: Harper, 1973), p. 20. Rilke's quote is found in *Letters to a Young Poet,* trans. M. D. Herter Norton (New York: Norton, 1954), p. 35;

emphasis is in original. On Christ "emptying" himself, see Philippians
2:7. The Nicholas Berdyaev comment is in *The Divine and the Human*
(London: Geoffrey Bles, 1949), p. 12. Levertov's image is found in her
poem "The Gift" in *Sands of the Well* (New York: New Directions,
1996), p. 18. Kierkegaard gave the four stages these names: aesthetic
(having fun); ethical (doing good) religious A, despair (burning out);
and religious B, grace (coming home).

6. THINKING YOUR WAY HOME

The McDonald epigraph is from *An Anthology,* ed. C. S. Lewis (New
York: Macmillan, 1974), p. 7. Cheever's is from *The Stories of John
Cheever* (New York: Ballantine, 1981), p. 543. Regarding "crucified
again and again," the writer to the Hebrews says of some believers that
"they are crucifying again the Son of God and are holding him up to
contempt" (Hebrews 6:6). Brian R. Greene's work is *The Elegant Universe: Superstrings, Hidden Dimensions, and the Quest for the Ultimate Theory* (New York: Norton, 1999), p. 15. On Pilate's question, see John
18:38. Howard Gardner explores the nexus of advanced theories and
childlike innocence in *Creating Minds: An Anatomy of Creativity Seen
Through the Lives of Freud, Einstein, Picasso, Stravinsky, Eliot, Graham and
Gandhi* (New York: Basic Books, 1993). The phrase "high-tech, high-
touch" comes from John Naisbitt's *Megatrends* (New York: Warner
Books, 1982). Leonard Sweet's comment is in *Quantum Spirituality: A
Postmodern Apologetic* (Dayton, Ohio: Whaleprints, 1989), p. 74. George
Gallup Jr. and Jim Castelli make the assertion in *The People's Religion:
American Faith in the 90s* (New York: Macmillan, 1989), as quoted in
Sweet's *Quantum Spirituality*. Beth Rohrbach-Perry's article, "The
Evolution of Creation," is in *Central Pa,* Sept. 2001, *21*(3), pp. 19–20.
Bishop Spong's story is from "Jesus for the 21st Century," lectures at
the Chautauqua Institution in western New York state, July 12–13,
2000. Ricoeur's phrase "second naïveté" is quoted in James W. Fowler,
*Stages of Faith: The Psychology of Human Development and the Quest for
Meaning* (San Francisco: HarperSanFrancisco, 1995), pp. 187–188, 197.
The T. S. Eliot lines are in "The Dry Salvages," from *Four Quartets*
(Orlando: Harcourt Brace, 1943), p. 44. "A Boy in Rome" is in *The
Stories of John Cheever* (New York: Knopf, 1978); the quoted passage is
on pp. 459–460, with italics added. For the sound and sun activities in
Reflection Exercise 11, I am indebted to Karl Bartsch's adaptation of

an experiment by former Dean Harold Schilling of Pennsylvania State University, a physicist widely known for research in ultrasonics and philosophy of science.

7. SWEATING YOUR WAY HOME

Hildegard of Bingen is cited in *The Quotable Woman,* ed. Elaine Partnow (New York: Meridian, 1993), Section 163:12, p. 48. The comment to Tom Beaudoin is from Beaudoin, *Virtual Faith: The Irreverent Spiritual Quest of Generation X* (San Francisco: Jossey-Bass, 1998) p. 14. Basava verse is from *The New Millennium Spiritual Journey* (Woodstock, Vt.: Skylight Paths, 1999), p. 21. Howard Gardner is discussed in *Frames of Mind: The Theory of Multiple Intelligences* (New York: Basic Books, 1983); and in *The Unschooled Mind: How Children Think and How Schools Should Teach* (New York: Basic Books, 1991), pp. 10–12. See also *Creating Minds* (mentioned in connection with Gardner in the note for Chapter Six). "One who sings prays twice" is attributed to Augustine of Hippo, of the fourth century. The rebbe story is adapted from "A Mitzvah Gives Life" in Rabbi Eugene Labovitz and Annette Labovitz, *Time for My Soul: A Treasury of Stories for Our Holy Days,* (Northvale, N.J.: Jason Aronson, 1987), p. 240. Rabbi Heschel is quoted in Robert Greenleaf, *Servant Leadership* (New York: Paulist Press, 1977), p. 253.

PART TWO. WONDER HAPPENS

St. Gregory of Nyssa is quoted in Ernest Kurtz and Katherine Ketcham, *The Spirituality of Imperfection: Storytelling and the Journey to Wholeness* (New York: Bantam Books, 1994), chapter two, note 1, p. 30. The F. Scott Fitzgerald quote is from *The Great Gatsby* (New York, Scribner's Sons, 1953), p. 182. The dialog with Frodo and Gildor is found in J.R.R. Tolkien, *The Lord of the Rings* (New York: Houghton Mifflin, 1987) p. 93.

8. DREAMS, DAYDREAMS, AND DISCOVERY

The first epigraph is from *The Journals and Papers of Gerard Manley Hopkins,* ed. Humphry House, completed by Graham Storey (London: Oxford University Press, 1959), p. 105. See also *Spiritus: A Journal of Christian Spirituality,* 2001, *1*(2), p. 185. The Warhol epigraph is quoted in *Pathways for Pastors,* ed. Daryl Fleming, *8*(3), p. 6 (available from

Brook Lane Health Services, P.O. Box 1945, Hagerstown, MD 21742–1945). For the concept of the acorn, see James Hillman, *The Soul's Code: In Search of Character and Calling* (New York: Random House, 1996). For the proverbial Einstein story, see Walker Percy, *The Second Coming* (New York: Farrar, Straus, and Giroux, 1980), p. 123. On James Watt, see R. A. Brown and R. G. Luckcock, "Dreams, Daydreams and Discovery," *Journal of Chemical Education,* 1978, *55*(11). Wislawa Szymborska is quoted in Robert Kennedy, *Zen Gifts for Christians* (New York: Continuum, 2000), p. 22. Regarding Haile-Selassie's discovery, see *Time,* July 23, 2001, pp. 54–61. On Ella Fitzgerald, see Hillman, *The Soul's Code* (1996), p. 10. Annie Dillard's passage is from *The Writing Life* (New York: HarperCollins, 1990), pp. 75–76.

9. SERENDIPITY!

Waldman's epigraph is from "Voices of 2000" (editorial), *Christian Century,* Dec. 20–27, 2000, *117*(36). Adrienne Rich is quoted in John Fox, *Poetic Medicine: The Healing Art of Poem-Making* (New York: Putnam/Tarcher, 1997), p. 23. The comment by Harvey Cox is in *Fire from Heaven: The Rise of Pentecostal Spirituality and the Reshaping of Religion in the Twenty-First Century* (Reading, Mass.: Addison-Wesley, 1995), p. xv. The master and disciples' dialogue about the sunrise is paraphrased by the author from Anthony de Mello, *One Minute Wisdom* (New York: Doubleday, 1986), p. 11. "How could we sing . . ." is from Psalm 137:4. "The best lack all conviction . . ." is by William Butler Yeats, quoted in Robert Bly, James, Hillman, and Michael Meade, *The Rag and Boneshop of the Heart: A Poetry Anthology* (New York: HarperCollins, 1992), p. 216. For the Reflection Exercise on doing things the opposite way, I am indebted to Kang Yup Na, professor of religion and New Testament at Westminster College in New Wilmington, Pennsylvania. Na draws from his own Korean background and ancient Asian and biblical traditions.

10. SHOCK.

The epigraph by F. Scott Fitzgerald was published in "One Hundred False Starts," *Saturday Evening Post* (March 4, 1933), and can be found at www.memorablequotations.com/complete.htm. See Luke 13:1–5 on Jesus' words regarding the Galileans. Ann Weems's verse is in *Psalms of Lament* (Louisville: Westminster John Knox Press, 1995), p. xvii. To read Jesus' saying "the other left" in context, see Luke 17:34. For an alternative to LaHaye and Jenkins' biblical fiction in their *Left Behind* series (Tyndale House), see Bruce M. Metzger, *Breaking the Code: Understanding the Book of Revelation* (Nashville: Abingdon, 1993).

11. YOU ARE DUST. YOU ARE STARS!

The epigraph by David Whyte is in *Crossing the Unknown Sea: Work as a Pilgrimage of Identity* (New York: Riverhead, 2001), p. 79. Buechner's phrase, "moments of crazy, holy grace," is from *Sacred Journey* (New York: Walker, 1984), p. 20. Frank Lloyd Wright is quoted in Linda S. Waggoner, *Falling Water: Frank Lloyd Wright's Romance with Nature* (Falling Water, Western Pennsylvania Conservancy, in association with New York: Universe Publishing, 1996), p. 29. Rilke's quotation "I am the rest" is from "My Life is Not This Steeply Sloping Hour," from *Selected Poems of Rainer Maria Rilke*, edited and translated by Robert Bly (New York: HarperCollins, 1981).

12. INSIGHT IS NOT TRANSFERABLE

The epigraph by Socrates from the *Symposium* is from Diogenes Allen, "Wisdom of the World and God's," *Princeton Seminary Bulletin*, 2002, *23*(2), New Series, p. 198X. For more by Sharon Daloz Parks, see *Big Questions, Worthy Dreams: Mentoring Young Adults in Their Search for Meaning, Purpose, and Faith* (San Francisco: Jossey-Bass, 2000), pp. 137–138. This story of Socrates from the *Symposium* is adapted from Diogenes Allen, (source above). "Things seen are made from things unseen": see Hebrews 11:1–3, which speaks of the same concept as the kabalistic *yesh mit ayn*, something from nothing. The seeker and teacher dialogue is drawn from the parable of the Good Samaritan in Luke 10:25–37. On being a believer outside the church, see Diogenes Allen's very readable *Three Outsiders: Pascal, Kierkegaard, and Simone Weil* (Cambridge, Mass.: Cowley Publications, 1983). Sojourner Truth was an African American woman who tirelessly worked for freedom and justice of slaves and ex-slaves. G. K. Chesterton is quoted in Frederick and Mary Ann Brussat's *Spiritual Literacy: Reading the Sacred in Everyday Life* (New York: Scribner, 1996).

PART THREE. MYSTERY

The first epigraph is from Ernest Hemingway, *A Farewell to Arms* (New York: Scribners, 1957). The epigraph about struggle by Joan D. Chittister is in her book, *Scarred by Struggle, Transformed by Hope* (Grand Rapids: Eerdmans, 2003), p. 83. The epigraph from musician Keith Wilson was given in personal conversation.

13. THE MURDER OF MYSTERY

Gabriel Marcel's quotation can be found in Eugene Peterson, *The Contemplative Pastor* (Carol Stream, Ill.: Word, 1989), p. 72. See Wendell Berry, *Life Is a Miracle* (Washington, D.C.: Counterpoint, 2000), p. 36. William Wordsworth is quoted in Theodore Roszak, *The Making of a Counter Culture: Reflections on the Technocratic Society and Its Youthful Opposition* (Garden City, N.Y.: Anchor Books, 1969), p. 254. For texts "has broken down the dividing wall" and "this One is our peace" (author's adaptation) see Ephesians 2:14; for the "mystery of Christ" see Ephesians 3:3–6; Colossians 1:21. See R. D. Laing, *The Politics of Experience* (New York: Ballantine, 1967), p. 44. E. L. Doctorow's story is summarized from *Ragtime* (New York: Random House, 1975).

14. "YOU SHOULD SEE MT. ST. HELENS NOW!"

"Listen to Love, to love" is from Deuteronomy 6:4; see also Matthew 22:37–40.

15. THE MATRIX

Thich Nhat Hanh is quoted by Lance Woodruff in "Remembering Connections Through War and Peace," *inSpire* (Princeton Theological Seminary), Summer/Fall 2001, *6*(1), pp. 16–17. Joyce Rupp's work is *Praying Our Goodbyes* (Notre Dame, Ind.: Ave Maria Press, 1988), pp. 83–93. The quote on relinquishment is from Deepak Chopra, *Seven Spiritual Laws of Success: A Practical Guide to the Fulfillment of Your Dreams* (New York: New World Library, 1994), p. 60. Daniel Schorr's interview was on National Public Radio, "Morning Edition," May 3, 2001. Rebbe Nachman of Breslov is quoted in Cooper, *Silence, Sim-*

plicity, and Solitude (1992), p. 81. More on this theme is found in Thich Nhat Hanh, *Anger: Wisdom for Cooling the Flames* (New York: Riverhead Penguin, 2001). Lance Woodruff, *inSpire,* pp. 16–17. See Matthew 6:25–34. The Buddhist scripture on the "lovely lotus" is the *Dhammapada,* 58–59, quoted in *World Scripture: A Comparative Anthology of Sacred Texts,* ed. Andrew Wilson (St. Paul: Paragon House, 1995), p. 680.

16. BEAUTY

The epigraph by Margaret Mead is from her Prologue in *Blackberry Winter* (New York: Simon and Schuster, 1972). John Biggers's quotation is from Jason McGarvey, "Bigger Vision," *The Penn Stater,* 2001, vol. 88, no. 5, p. 36. Ma is quoted in Ruth Ann Ridley, "From Chaos to Cosmos: The Perseverance of J. S. Bach," *Christianity and the Arts,* 1999, vol. 6, no. 3, p. 11. The Pietist quote is in Ridley (1999), also p. 11. The fragment of Vincent van Gogh's journal entry is in the *Columbia Dictionary of Quotations* (New York: Columbia University Press, 1993); his letter to Theo is in Letters 3:27, June 25, 1889, quoted by Kathleen Erickson in "Starry Night: Van Gogh's Spiritual Autobiography," *Christianity and the Arts,* 2000, vol. 7, no.3, pp. 21–26. The "morphology of human senses" is in Suzanne Langer, *Philosophy in a New Key* (Cambridge: Harvard University Press, 1957). Eliot's quote is also in "The Dry Salvages" (1971), p. 44. Paul's quote is from 2 Corinthians 12:9. See Barbara Kingsolver, *The Poisonwood Bible* (New York: HarperCollins, 1998), p. 276.

17. GESTURE

Mohandas Gandhi is quoted in Laurence G. Boldt, *Zen and the Art of Making a Living* (New York: Penguin Books, 1993), p. 134. Writer Joan Lipscomb Solomon made the statement about "gesture embraces all" in a writing seminar I taught at Chautauqua Institution, New York, July 2002. Albert Camus's *Lyrical and Critical Essays* are cited in R. M. Brown, *Creative Dislocation* (Philadelphia: 1980), p. 66. On the anointing, see Matthew 26:10 (RSV). The Gandhi story is adapted from *The Essential Gandhi: An Anthology of His Life, Work and Ideas,* ed. Louis Fischer (New York: Vintage Books, 1962), pp. 35–37. Rosa Parks story (with Jim Haskins) is told in *Rosa Parks: My Story* (New York: Dial Books, 1992). For Victor Hugo and *Les Miserables,* see the translation by Charles Wilbour, abridged by James K. Robinson (New York: Ballantine Books, 1987), pp. 38–39.

18. EMPTINESS

The first epigraph is by K. M. George, *The Silent Roots* (see chapter 3), p. 58. Nicholas Berdyaev's epigraph is in *The Divine and the Human* (see chapter 5), p. 12. On the opening discussion, see "Fashions for the Times—The Pilgrimage Issue," *New York Times Magazine,* Aug. 18, 2002, Part 2. Regarding bipolar disorder, "Young and Bipolar," by Jeffrey Kluger with Sora Song, is the feature article in *Time,* Aug. 19, 2002, pp. 38–47. "Let there be light!": see Genesis 1:1–3. For more on a Christian interpretation of *kenosis,* see Jurgen Moltmann, *God in Creation: An Ecological Doctrine of Creation* (London: SCM Press, 1985), p. 86. On Jesus equaling God, see Philippians 2:7. Donald W. Mitchell's discussion is in *Spirituality and Emptiness: The Dynamics of Spiritual Life in Buddhism and Christianity* (New York: Paulist Press, 1991), p. 189. Mitchell's book provides a thorough treatment of Buddhist Christian concepts. The Dr. Seuss book is *Oh, The Places You'll Go!* by Theodore S. Geisel and Audrey S. Geisel (New York: Random House, 1990). On calamitous distraction, in *Traveling Mercies* Ann Lamott tells us of the idea, indirectly from the Dalai Lama, of "something big and lovely that wants to get itself born"—something that needs you to be distracted. Heisenberg's discourse with his assistant is recounted in Wayne Muller, *Sabbaths* (New York: Bantam Books, 1999), p. 190. On instances of dumbfounded silence, see Isaiah 6:1–10 and Luke 1:5–25. On Moses hiding in the shadow, see Exodus 20:21. "Colorless green ideas" is from Noam Chomsky, *Syntactic Structures* (The Hague: Mouton, 1957), chapter 2. On Nicodemus coming by night to be born anew, see John 3:3 and 3:7. The Greek word for anew *(anothen)* can also be translated "again" or "from above," "from top to bottom." 1 Peter 1:3 also speaks of this "new birth." On Paul's blackout period, see Galatians 1:17–18. Paul says he retreated to Arabia and then returned to Damascus; only after three years did he go up to Jerusalem and engage in active ministry. Karen Armstrong discusses al-Ghazzali in *A History of God: The 4,000-Year Quest of Judaism, Christianity and Islam* (New York: Ballantine Books, 1993), pp. 187–188. On chaos theory and depression, see John E. Nelson, M.D., and Andrea Nelson, Psy.D., eds., *Sacred Sorrows* (New York: Putnam, 1996), p. 129. Camus's comment is from *Return to Tipasa,* quoted in *Bartlett's Familiar Quotations: Sixteenth Edition,* Justin Kaplan, ed. (Boston, Mass.: Little Brown and Co., 1992), p. 732. Andrew Solomon's work is *The Noonday Demon: An Atlas of Depression* (New York: Scribner, 2001), pp. 16–17. "Night Demons," by the author, was published in *Presence, The Journal of Spiritual Directors International,* 1998, vol. 4, no. 3, p. 3. It was also published in Kent Ira Groff, *Journeymen: A Spiritual Guide for Men (and for Women Who Want to Understand Them)* (Nashville: Upper Room Books, 1999), pp. 88–89. The summary of the empty tomb story is from John 20:1–18. Solomon's comment on "the opposite of depression" is in *The Noonday Demon* (2001), p. 443. *Space for God* is the title of an excellent book for personal or group study and prayer, by Don Postema (Grand Rapids: CRC, 1983).

19. SEX, MYSTICISM, AND WORK

The epigraph by Alan Jones is in *Exploring Spiritual Direction: An Essay on Christian Friendship* (Boston: Cowley, 1982, 1989), p. 73. The epigraph by W. Paul Jones is in *Teaching a Dead Bird to Sing: Living the Hermit Life Without and Within* (Brewster, Mass.: Paraclete Press, 2002), p. 178. The Meister Eckhart epigraph is from Matthew Fox, *Creation Spirituality* (Santa Fe: Bear and Company, 1983), p. 178. For examples or "romancing the divine," see the Song of Songs in the Bible, the Jewish Kabala tradition, and Christian writings of John of the Cross. In varied ways, it is found in the Tantric tradition of Hinduism. In the Sufi tradition, see Rumi, *The Glance,* trans. Coleman Barks with Nevit Ergin (New York: Viking, 1999). On John of the Cross, see *Selected Writings,* ed. K. Kavanaugh, (New York: Paulist Press, 1987), pp. 55–57. On the gift of caring for creation, see Genesis 1:26–28 and 2:15. See the first creation story in Genesis 1, especially 1:31; the second is in Genesis 2:25; and for the effect of "sin" on creation, see 3:16, 19. On creativity gestating in silence, see Tillie Olson, *Silences* (New York: Dell, 1978), pp. 137–138.

PART FOUR. HOW SHALL WE THEN LIVE?

Peter Byrne, S.J., composed the epigraph "We Are Simply Asked" for his ordination; it was later set to music by Jim Strathdee (Desert Flower Music, Ridgecrest, Calif. 93555). Howard Thurman is quoted in a sidebar in the alumni magazine of Candler School of Theology

(Emory University), in the article "Dwelling More Fully in God," by Jeremy Hajdu-Paulen, *Candler Connection*, Spring 2001.

20. PLAYFUL PROJECTS FOR SERIOUS PURPOSES

Jesus' saying about a child is in Mark 9:33. The Goethe quote is found in Annie Dillard, *The Writing Life* (see chapter 8), p. 1. Eliot's well-known verse is in "Little Gidding," in *Four Quartets* (Orlando: Harvest/Harcourt Brace, 1971), p. 59. Gorky's statement is from his autobiographical trilogy *My Childhood* (1913), quoted in *Merriam-Webster's Encyclopedia of Literature* (Springfield, Mass.: Merriam-Webster, 1995), p. 479.

21. LIVE AS IF YOU HAD A THOUSAND YEARS TO LIVE, LIVE AS IF YOU MUST DIE TOMORROW

The chapter title is adapted from *Testimonies of the Life, Character, Revelations and Doctrines of Our Ever Blessed Mother Ann Lee* (Hancock, Mass.: Josiah Talcott, Jr., 1816). The epigraph by Niels Bohr is quoted in Parker Palmer, *The Courage to Teach* (San Francisco: Jossey-Bass, 1998), p. 62. On Romero's last words, see J. Matthew Ashley, "Contemplation and Prophetic Action," *Bulletin for the Study of Christian Spirituality*, 2000, vol. 8, no. 1. The Bono cover story was in *Time*, Mar. 4, 2002. The review and quotations about Bruce Springsteen are taken from the *New York Times*, July 14, 2002, Sect. 2, pp. 1 and 28. John Newton's dream story is recounted in David G. Benner, *Care of Souls: Revisioning Christian Nurture and Counsel* (Grand Rapids: Baker Books, 1998), p. 168.

22. CHOCOLÁT AND SPIDER-MAN

David Steindl-Rast's epigraph is from *Gratefulness: The Heart of Prayer* (New York: Paulist Press, 1984), pp. 20–21. Steindl-Rast is also quoted in *Spiritus: A Journal of Christian Spirituality*, Fall 2001, *1*(2), p. 185. Joseph Campbell's repeated theme "follow your bliss" is found in *The Power of Myth*, with Bill Moyers (New York: Doubleday, 1988), pp. 117-121, 148, and 229. Reinhold Niebuhr is quoted (see sidebar) in Mark I. Pinsky, *The Gospel According to the Simpsons* (Louisville, Ky.: Westminster John Knox Press, 2001), p. 5. Dag Hammarskjöld's quote is from *Markings*, tr. by Lief Sjöberg and W. H. Auden (New York: Alfred A. Knopf, 1964), p. 89. The story of James Loder is from his *The*

Transforming Moment: Understanding Convictional Experiences (San Francisco: HarperSanFrancisco, 1981).

23. LISTEN TO LOVE, TO LOVE

The Mechtild of Magdeburg epigraph is from Matthew Fox, *Creation Spirituality*, p. 88. Brother Lawrence's epigraph is in *The Practice of the Presence of God*, p. 97. The Susan Gibson story is from Richard Scheinin, "Finding God in Silicone Valley," *Christian Century*, 2001, *118*(22), pp. 18–25. Nathaniel Hawthorne's story "The Great Stone Face" is summarized here from *The Complete Novels and Selected Tales of Nathaniel Hawthorne*, ed. Norman Holmes Pearson (New York: Modern Library, 1937), pp. 1170–1184. Wallace Stevens is quoted in John Fox, *Poetic Medicine: The Healing Art of Poem-Making* (New York: Tarcher/Putnam, 1977), p. 34. On the Christian "imitation of Christ," cp. Leviticus 19:2 ("Be holy as I the Lord your God am holy") with Paul in Ephesians 5:1: "Be imitators of God." In other texts, Paul speaks of the same idea as a call to "imitate Christ" (1 Corinthians 1:1). Charles Hartshorne's quotation is from his book *Creative Synthesis and Philosophic Method* (La Salle, Ill.: Open Court, 1970), p. 303.

24. SINGLING IN COMMUNITY

"God's own image ..." is in Genesis 1:26–28. Thurman's quote about being true to one's own grain is verified by Luther Smith, Candler School of Theology. (The Thurman quote appeared on the bulletin of Fifth Avenue Presbyterian Church in New York City on Oct. 1, 2001.) On connecting being alone with being all one, see Debra K. Farrington's meaningful book of meditative readings for single persons, *One Like Jesus: Conversations on the Single Life* (Chicago: Loyola Press, 1999). Regarding the *"YHWH"* poem, see Genesis 4: 1–16; "The Mark of Cain" was published on the cover of *Presbyterian Outlook*, 1994, *176*(11). Joyce Rupp's book *Praying Our Goodbyes* (1988) was cited in the notes for Chapter Fifteen; it is an invaluable resource for personal and communal healing.

25. DANCING YOUR WAY HOME AGAIN

Kierkegaard's epigraph is found in Ernest Kurtz and Katherine Ketcham, *The Spirituality of Imperfection* (New York: Bantam Books, 1992), p. 153. On *Sankofa*, see Grenaé D. Dudley and Carlyle Fielding

Stewart III, *Sankofa: Celebrations for the African American Church* (Cleveland: United Church Press, 1997), p. 9. André Dubus is quoted from "A Father's Story," *Listening for God, Vol. 2,* ed. Paula J. Carlson and Peter S. Hawkins (Minneapolis: Augsburg Fortress, 1996), p. 147. For the discussion at the Zulu phrase, I am indebted to Thulani Ndlazi, pastor-theologian in South Africa, and to South African Graham Cyster in the United States for this discussion. See as well John S. Mbiti, *An Introduction to African Religions and Philosophy* (Oxford, England: Heinemann International, 1989). The epigraph and quote from Alex Haley is in *Roots: The Saga of an American Family* (Garden City, N.Y.: Doubleday, 1976), p. 134. The comment on surfing is from Oswald Chambers, *My Utmost for His Highest* (New York: Dodd, Mead, 1961), p. 67. Jesus' analog of the comment from Victor Frankl is in Matthew 6:22 (my translation from the Greek). Amy Spindler writes in the *New York Times Magazine,* Aug. 22, 2002. Hammarskjöld's quote "the world of action" is in *Markings,* p. 122. The Estonian proverb is quoted in Laurence G. Boldt, *Zen and the Art of Making a Living* (New York: Penguin, 1993), p. 33. "Receiving life, dying to self-deceit, and giving back": the New Testament shows us that such genuine yearnings of God-seekers can begin with awareness of the Divine and lead to a personal experience of Christ. See Acts 10:4, 30, 34–35: the Gentile Cornelius has been praying, and then Peter realizes that God shows no favoritism but hears the prayers of all. On the clearness committee, see Parker Palmer's article by that title in *Weavings* (Nov.–Dec. 1988), vol. 3.

P.S. FOR ONCE OR MAYBE CHRISTIANS

The epigraph on George MacLeod is in Carl F. Burke, *God Is for Real, Man* (New York: Association Press, 1966), Preface. I have adapted *churchmen* to *Christians.* The story of Bud and the inner-city church is summarized from Thomas R. Hawkins, *The Learning Congregation* (Louisville: Westminster John Knox Press, 1997), p. 131. The story of the atheist coalition meeting on Easter is told by John Galloway, a Presbyterian minister in Wayne, Pennsylvania. Albert Schweitzer's statement (paraphrased by author) is in *The Quest of the Historical Jesus* (Baltimore: Johns Hopkins University Press, 1998), p. 403.

BIBLIOGRAPHY

SPIRITUALITY FOR TODAY'S NEW ADULTS

Tom Beaudoin. *Virtual Faith: The Irreverent Spiritual Quest of Generation X.* San Francisco: Jossey-Bass, 1998.

Editors of Skylight Paths. *The New Millennium Spiritual Journey: Change Your Life—Develop Your Spiritual Priorities with Help from Today's Most Inspiring Spiritual Teachers.* Woodstock, Vt.: Skylight Paths, 1999.

Niles Elliot Goldstein (ed.). *Spiritual Manifestos: Visions for Renewed Religious Life in America from Young Spiritual Leaders of Many Faiths.* Preface by Martin Marty. Woodstock, Vt.: Skylight Paths, 1999.

Brett Hoover. *Losing Your Religion, Finding Your Faith: Spirituality for Young Adults.* New York: Paulist, 1998.

Scotty McLennan. *Finding Your Religion: When the Faith You Grew Up with Has Lost Its Meaning.* Introduction by Garry Trudeau. San Francisco: HarperSanFrancisco, 1999.

Sharon Daloz Parks. *Big Questions, Worthy Dreams: Mentoring Young Adults in Their Search for Meaning, Purpose, and Faith.* San Francisco: Jossey-Bass, 2001.

Jon M. Sweeney (ed.). *God Within: Our Spiritual Future—As Told by Today's New Adults.* Woodstock, Vt.: Skylight Paths, 2001.

BRIDGE BOOKS

Anthony de Mello, *Sadhana: A Way to God: Christian Exercises in Eastern Form.* New York: Doubleday, 1978, 1984.

Paul Hawker. *Soul Survivor: A Spiritual Quest through 40 Days and 40 Nights of Mountain Solitude.* Kelowna, British Columbia: Northstone, 1998.

Robert Kennedy. *Zen Gifts for Christians.* New York: Continuum, 2000.

Thich Nhat Hanh. *Living Buddha, Living Christ.* New York: Riverhead Books, 1995.

John O'Donohue. *Anam Cara: A Book of Celtic Wisdom.* New York: Cliff Street Books (HarperCollins), 1998.

SPIRITUAL FICTION

Paulo Coelho. *The Alchemist.* (Clifford E. Landers, trans.). New York: HarperPerennial, 1998.

Zora Neale Hurston. *Their Eyes Were Watching God.* New York: HarperPerennial, 1990. (Originally published 1937.)

Mark Salzman. *Lying Awake.* New York: Alfred A. Knopf, 2000.

SACRED POETRY

Patricia Hampl (ed.). *Burning Bright: An Anthology of Sacred Poetry.* New York: Ballantine Books, 1995.

FILMS AND SPIRITUALITY

Robert K. Johnston. *Reel Spirituality: Theology and Film in Dialogue.* Grand Rapids, Mich.: Baker, 2000.

Edward McNulty. *Praying the Movies: Daily Meditations from Classic Films.* Louisville: Geneva, 2001.

RECOVERING FROM SPIRITUAL BURNOUT

Marcus Borg. *The God We Never Knew: Beyond Dogmatic Religion to a More Authentic Contemporary Faith.* San Francisco: HarperSanFrancisco, 1997.

Mary Tuomi Hammond. *Church for the Dechurched: Mending a Damaged Faith.* St. Louis: Chalice, 2001.

Anne Lamott. *Traveling Mercies: Some Thoughts on Faith.* New York: Pantheon, 1999.

Brian D. McLaren. *A New Kind of Christian: A Tale of Two Friends on a Spiritual Journey.* San Francisco: Jossey-Bass, 2001.

John Shelby Spong. *A New Christianity for a New World: Why Traditional Faith Is Dying and How a New Faith Is Being Born.* San Francisco: HarperSanFrancisco, 2002.

Philip Yancey. *Soul Survivor: How My Faith Survived the Church.* New York: Doubleday, 2001.

Pamela Dickey Young. *Christ in a Post-Christian World: How Can We Believe in Jesus Christ When Those Around Us Believe Differently—or Not At All?* Minneapolis: Fortress, 1995.

THE AUTHOR

Kent Ira Groff is a pilgrim of East and West who loves to connect with fellow journeyers, learn from them, hear their stories, and experience a deeper purpose for life on this out-of-balance planet. Since 1989, his retreat ministry has taken him to conference centers, college campuses, seminaries, prisons, workplaces, and health-related institutions across the United States and abroad. He has led events for the Upper Room Spiritual Formation Academy, Chautauqua Institution, New York; Princeton Theological Seminary; Allenwood Federal Prison in Pennsylvania; the Washington National Cathedral; and at sites in Europe, Africa, India, Central America, and Canada. Previously he served Presbyterian congretions for twenty years, and as a chaplain.

As a minister's minister and a seeker's guide, he describes his work as one beggar showing other beggars where to find bread. His writings include *Active Spirituality: A Guide for Seekers and Ministers; The Soul of Tomorrow's Church;* and *Journeymen: A Spiritual Guide for Men (and for Women Who Want to Understand Them).*

A graduate of Pennsylvania State University, trained in theology at Princeton and Chicago, and in spirituality at Shalem Institute, Bethesda, Maryland, Groff serves as founding mentor of Oasis Ministries for Spiritual Development, Camp Hill,

Pennsylvania and as adjunct professor at nearby Lancaster Theological Seminary. He is an associate of Holy Cross Monastery,
West Park, New York. Previously he served as a minister of
Presbyterian congregations for two decades. He has a passion to
connect with seekers and find common ground. To schedule a
conference or retreat, contact the author at Oasis Ministries,
419 Deerfield Road, Camp Hill, Pennsylvania 17011. Web site:
www.oasismin.org.

CREDITS

All scripture quotations, unless otherwise noted, are from the New Revised Standard Version of the Bible, copyright ©1989 by the Division of Christian Education of the National Council of the Churches of Christ in the United States of America. Used by permission.

All poetry not otherwise noted is by the author.

Texts from the *Bhagavad Gita: The Song of God;* the *Koran;* and the *Tao Te Ching,* unless otherwise noted, are taken from *World Scripture: A Comparative Anthology of Sacred Texts,* A Project of the International Religious Foundation, ed. Andrew Wilson (St. Paul, Minn.: Paragon House, 1995).

Lyrics from "Scarlet Begonias" by Robert Hunter are used by permission of Ice Nine Publishing Co.

Lyrics from "I'll Have to Say I Love You in a Song" are written by Jim Croce. Copyright © 1973 (Renewed) Croce Publishing/Time in a Bottle (ASCAP). Used by permission. ALL RIGHTS RESERVED. Permission for world rights by Larry Moelis.

Excerpt from "His Kind of Heroes, His Kind of Songs" by Jon Pareles. Copyright © 2002 by The New York Times Co. Reprinted with permission.

Excerpt from "Everything About Warhol But the Sex" by Holland Cotter. Copyright © 2002 by The New York Times Co. Reprinted with permission.

Excerpt from "The Pilgrimage Issue" by Amy Spindler. Copyright © 2002 by *New York Times Magazine.* Reprinted with permission.

Excerpt from SANDS OF THE WELL, copyright © 1996 by Denise Levertov. Reprinted by permission of New Directions Publishing Corp.

Excerpts from "The Dry Salvages" in FOUR QUARTERS, copyright © 1941 by T.S. Eliot and renewed 1969 by Esme Valerie Eliot,

X